INTRODUCED
AA International Convention with Al-Anon participation
July 2, 1955 • St. Louis, MO

"The message of the Al-Anon Family Groups is a simple story of hope."

RE-INTRODUCED—CLASSIC EDITION
AA International Convention with Al-Anon participation
June 29 - July 2, 2000 • Minneapolis, MN

The
Al-Anon Family
Groups

Classic Edition

Al-Anon Family Groups
Hope for Families and Friends of Alcoholics

The Al-Anon Family Groups are a fellowship of relatives and friends of alcoholics who share their experience, strength, and hope in order to solve their common problems. We believe alcoholism is a family illness and that changed attitudes can aid recovery.

Al-Anon is not allied with any sect, denomination, political entity, organization, or institution; does not engage in any controversy; neither endorses nor opposes any cause. There are no dues for membership. Al-Anon is self-supporting through its own voluntary contributions.

Al-Anon has but one purpose: to help families of alcoholics. We do this by practicing the Twelve Steps, by welcoming and giving comfort to families of alcoholics, and by giving understanding and encouragement to the alcoholic.

For information and catalog of literature write World Service Office for Al-Anon and Alateen:

Al-Anon Family Group Headquarters, Inc.
1600 Corporate Landing Parkway
Virginia Beach, VA 23454-5617
757-563-1600 / Fax 757-563-1655
www.al-anon.alateen.org • e-mail: wso@al-anon.org

Library of Congress Catalog Card No. 84-7019
ISBN 0-910034-36-2

Publishers Cataloging in Publication

Al-Anon Family Groups—Classic Edition
includes index

1. Alcoholism—psychological aspects 2. Alcoholics—Family relationship 3. Alcoholics—Rehabilitation 4. Children of Alcoholics 5. Adult children of alcoholics 6. Al-Anon Family Group Headquarters, Inc.

Approved by
World Service Conference
Al-Anon Family Groups

1-25m-00-10.00   B-5   Printed in the USA

PREFACE

When *The Al-Anon Family Groups* was first written, Al-Anon had very little literature and relied on the founding wisdom of Alcoholics Anonymous (AA). Our early pioneers at the first World Service Conference in 1961 saw the value of unity through our literature, and like AA established that Al-Anon would produce "Conference Approved Literature" (CAL). Through the leadership of our early members, and the ensuing development of the "CAL process," Al-Anon now has its own wealth of literature offering help and hope to families and friends of alcoholics. The journey from then to now is fascinating as well as historical.

Lois W., Al-Anon co-founder, in *Lois Remembers*, (p. 180) stated:"... for two years [1953-1955] we had struggled to prepare our first book, *The Al-Anon Family Groups*. With Bill's help I wrote the first draft of what we thought was going to be a pamphlet. Then Trudy M., a short-time but most capable volunteer, with Margaret's [Margaret D., the first Forum Editor] help, made a connected manuscript out of it. Bill and I went over it again and added some material. Ralph B., an AA writer, edited it, and we sent mimeographed copies to groups selected at random. Many of their suggestions and stories were so good that the pamphlet grew into a book. Finally at the 1955 AA International Convention in St. Louis (where Al-Anon participated in workshops), the multi-authored book made its appearance . . ."

"The original work was called a 'Handbook,' and covered all the basics—how to start a group, the Steps, the Traditions, solving group problems, and personal stories" (*Inside Al-Anon*, April/May 1987).

At the January 1959 Board meeting, the Literature Committee reported, "a start will soon be made . . . on the revision of the book . . ." In April of 1960 the Board reported ". . . in an effort to 'appeal to a wider audience,' the title was changed to *Living With an Alcoholic.*"

"With Al-Anon growth and a newly formed Conference,[1] revisions were needed to mirror in print the changing images [of] the fellowship. While the principles of the program, the Steps, and the Traditions didn't change, their interpretation and use changed as the fellowship grew from wives of AA members to include men and women of a wide range of relationships to the alcoholic—parents, teenagers, adult children, lovers, brothers and sisters, co-workers, etc." (*Inside Al-Anon*, April/May 1987)

The circle has widened over the years to include all those who have lived with alcoholism: husbands, friends, those living with active alcoholism, widows and widowers, gay and lesbian partners and members of AA who have been affected by someone else's drinking.

"By 1984, the Conference had come full circle and approved reinstating its original title, *Al-Anon Family Groups*"[2] (*Inside Al-Anon*, April/May 1987).

The in-town Literature Committee[3] minutes from 1984 tell us, "At her request, [the staff] visited Lois to seek her input regarding the possible revision and expansion of the *Al-Anon Family Groups* book. They asked her if there had ever been a decision <u>not</u> to have a basic book as complete as AA's. Lois said, in fact, that early members had used everything they had that seemed worthwhile at the time and produced these sharings in the original book *The Al-Anon Family Groups*. There were many pioneers who didn't have the opportunity to include their stories. She also felt that many young people's stories are missing as experiences and that it might be a good idea to include material on how Al-Anon works. Sponsorship was another topic she thought deserved coverage."

---

1. In 1961, the first Al-Anon World Service Conference was held.

2. The word "The" was dropped from the title,

3. This Literature Committee was composed of Al-Anon members from the local New York area who met monthly,

In 1986 the Conference set a new direction by deciding to expand the basic text of *Al-Anon Family Groups*. Over the next few years the fellowship provided input, and members of the Literature Committee reviewed a multitude of ideas on how to revise the book. Debate concluded with three possible revision directions for the 1990 Conference to consider. In the final analysis, the Conference voted to rescind the 1986 Conference motion, leave the book as it was, and develop a totally new book on Al-Anon today. This was published in 1995 as *How Al-Anon Works for Families & Friends of Alcoholics*.

Over the years, use of *Al-Anon Family Groups* declined as newer books were introduced. In January 1995 the Board of Trustees, as prudent managers of the fellowship's resources, voted to discontinue further printing of the book. At the April 1995 World Service Conference members recognized the legal rights of the Board of Trustees in making business decisions, yet expressed desire for continued printings. The Conference additionally approved a motion requesting the Board "notify all Conference members of its intent to discontinue any hard/softcover books one year prior to the discontinuance or failure to print." As inventory at the WSO was totally depleted, the Board (acknowledging the Conference's direction) authorized an immediate reprint of the book. The Budget Committee and Executive Committee further authorized the publication of the book in soft cover for the first time.

Despite declining orders for the book, the 1998 World Service Conference passed the following motion: "Upon depletion of current stock, the World Service Conference gives the World Service Office conceptual approval to return to the use of the original text of *Al-Anon Family Groups* (with appropriate footnotes and annotations) when reprinting *Al-Anon Family Groups*, if financially feasible."

This book is the end product of that motion. The text (pp. 11-100) is as it was written in 1955. There are footnotes denoting changes within the fellowship over the years. Appendix II features chapters that were added in subsequent editions and presented as they were when they were introduced the first time. Text changes in later years are not cited. Policy changes have also been noted in the text or in Appendix II. *Al-Anon Family Groups* was indexed for the first time in 1986. The index to this publication also includes references to all footnotes, annotations and the additional appendix.

The original text reflects the use of wording and terminology in the context of 1955. For example, throughout the text the term "Family Group(s)" is used; today we would say "Al-Anon" or "Al-Anon Family Group(s)." The "Clearing House" referred to in the original text is today known as Al-Anon Family Group Headquarters, Inc., Al-Anon's World Service Office. Many references are made to Alcoholics Anonymous (AA) and to AA literature. Though we cooperate with AA, we are a separate entity, and AA literature is no longer used in Al-Anon meetings.

Al-Anon has come a long way, evolving from a handful of isolated "Family Groups" in the shadow of AA, to an independent fellowship with 30,000 groups in over 112 countries worldwide (as of 2000). We have a wealth of literature, service materials and a World Wide Web site available to us today; yet as Al-Anon nears its 50th anniversary in 2001, the words of our co-founders and early pioneers remain valued and relevant. We hope the reader will savor this journey into the past and see clearly how Al-Anon's principles and single purpose have remained constant through the years, continuing to provide support and encouragement to families and friends of alcoholics everywhere.

all good wishes to you in Al-Anon

Lois

Inscription by Lois W., Al-Anon co-founder, found in a 1966 edition.

NOTE[4]

Throughout this pamphlet[5] generally, except in the chapter to husbands, we have used the masculine and feminine pronouns, respectively, to represent the alcoholic and his mate, since there are at least five or six times as many alcoholic men as women.

By the term "non-alcoholic" we mean not a teetotaler but someone without a personal alcoholic problem.

THE AL-ANON FAMILY GROUPS
A Guide for the Families of Problem Drinkers

1955 Original Edition with Footnotes and Annotations added in 2000
Copyright 2000

Published by
The Al-Anon Family Groups Headquarters, Inc.
A World Clearing House for serving the Families of Alcoholics
Anonymous and other Problem Drinkers

---

4. See Appendix II, #1 for revised note from 1960 edition.
5. With the second printing of this book in March 1956, the word "pamphlet" was changed to "book."

CONTENTS

6. Appendix II, p.101, provides a separate Table of Contents regarding supplementary information added after the first printing of this book in 1955.

THE FAMILY GROUP PROGRAM

Introduction

THE AL-ANON FAMILY GROUPS are a fellowship of the wives, husbands, relatives and friends of members of Alcoholics Anonymous and of problem drinkers generally, who are banded together to solve their common problems of fear, insecurity, lack of understanding of the alcoholic, and of the warped personal lives resulting from alcoholism. The primary purpose of the Al-Anon Family Groups is to carry their helpful experience in gaining greater happiness to the non-alcoholic who seeks personal understanding of the problem of alcoholism and how to cope with its consequences.

The message of the Al-Anon Family Groups is a simple story of hope. It is the story of men and women who once felt hopelessly alone and powerless to deal with the alcoholism of their loved ones. Today these men and women no longer feel lost or lonely. They have learned that there are simple things that they can do to help themselves and their alcoholic partners.

Many who are now in Family Groups have already seen their loved ones achieve sobriety through AA; they know that life with a sober alcoholic can present special problems, too. Others still have active problem drinkers in their homes. All members share the friendly bond of men and women who have turned from defeat and frustration to a new way of life in which positive, constructive thinking is the keynote.

Only you yourself can decide whether the Family Group program can prove helpful to you. If your decision is in the affirmative, the Family Groups welcome and invite you to share their fellowship and the rich rewards that are certain to follow.[7]

---

7. In 1960 the introduction was totally rewritten. See Appendix II, #2 for the revised text which includes the Serenity Prayer.

Historical Foreword[8]

This is the story of a unique society that has its beginnings in two very great needs and desires. It is the story of thousands of men and women who—like yourself, perhaps—sought two things. Non-alcoholics themselves, they wanted to understand and help the problem drinker in their family, or one close to them. More importantly, they sought *for themselves* a new approach to living. They recognized that alcoholism can twist the emotions and thinking of wives and husbands of alcoholics, too. They wanted to examine their own thinking and behavior and, where necessary, change those into more constructive channels.

Like the alcoholic himself, they sought a program of recovery and growth. They wanted to recover the ability to think clearly about the everyday problems of marriage, family relationships and community life. They wanted to recover from the skepticism, fears and doubts that had sometimes colored their thinking during their association with alcoholic partners.

In the past few decades, there have been great changes in the public attitude toward alcoholism. Among many approaches to the problem, one of the most successful is that of the fellowship of Alcoholics Anonymous. Members of AA achieve sobriety by following a fundamentally simple program. They face up realistically to the fact that they are powerless over alcohol. They recognize the importance of honesty and humility in dealing with life's problems. Next, they offer their experience and encouragement freely to anyone who turns to them in an effort to achieve sobriety. And finally, they rely for guidance upon a Power greater than themselves. AA has grown steadily since its founding in 1935 until today there are an estimated 150,000 sober alcoholics in more than 5,000 groups in about 50 countries.[9]

---

8. This heading was changed in the 1960 edition to "How Al-Anon Came to Be," and the foreword was substantially rewritten.

9. As of December 31, 1998, there were 98,710 AA groups worldwide with an estimated membership of two million in 150 countries.

In these local groups all over the world, ex-problem drinkers exchange experiences and viewpoints. At the end of the meetings, they mingle informally and make a special effort to welcome and assist newcomers.

The Family Group idea is nearly as old as Alcoholics Anonymous itself. In the pioneering days of AA—1935-41—wives and relatives of the recovering alcoholics began to realize they still had a common problem, even though their partners had sobered up.

It was a serious dilemma which had two aspects. Wives saw they needed a deeper understanding of what alcohol had done to their partners. This much they could, of course, learn at AA meetings. But the more difficult problem was to understand what alcohol had done to them, the non-alcoholics. Just how had living with an alcoholic warped and deformed their own personalities? What did this have to do with the fact that it was often difficult to re-establish a happy home life with the AA member? And if this was the condition, what could the non-alcoholic partners themselves do about it?

Of course, they could go to AA meetings and listen. Each of them could try to apply the Twelve Steps to his or her life. A return to more intense church and community work could be made. All of these ideas were tried, but a gap seemed to remain that simply would not be filled.

Therefore, in some of the early AA groups the non-alcoholics began to have meetings of their own to discuss their problems, the damage alcoholism had done them and what they could do about it. Though they had no set program or distinct society of their own, the results were beneficial indeed. Without knowing it, they were laying the foundation of the present day Al-Anon Groups.

For some years, though, the Family Group idea did not keep pace with the growth of Alcoholics Anonymous. It was almost lost sight of during the great expansion that began with Jack Alexander's famous article about AA in the *Saturday Evening Post* in 1941. In many localities, AA members frowned on the idea, feeling Family Groups could become gossip clubs or divert AA from its main purpose.

Nevertheless, the underlying problem of difficult family relations persisted. This condition was aggravated by the feeling of non-alcoholic members of families that they never could quite belong to AA, and this was multiplied many times by thousands of new families appearing on the scene who found that in many places the AAs held mostly closed meetings, which excluded them.

Because of the universal feeling of need for some specific program for their own development, spontaneously, in several far separated sections of this country and Canada, special meetings for families again began to evolve. Early groups sprang up in Toronto, Chicago, San Pedro, (California); Richmond, (Virginia) and elsewhere. This time the insight on what had really happened to the families of alcoholics was clearer. Also many wives had had time to try out the AA program on themselves. They found it worked for them, also. Regular meetings with well-conceived programs developed.

As these pioneer groups became well established, they helped to start other groups. By 1949, the pent-up desire on the part of non-alcoholic partners to make a better life for their families really broke into the open. In this year, the AA General Headquarters[10] received scores of inquiries from distracted wives and husbands of alcoholics. Many of these asked how they could start Family Groups. Some 50 Family Groups applied for listing in the AA directory.[11] But AA Headquarters, serving AA only, saw that it could not meet the needs of this new movement.

To meet this requirement for service, a number of husbands and wives of AA members in and about New York City formed a committee which later became the Al-Anon Family Groups Clearing House. The new movement mushroomed rapidly. With the establishment of a post office box, the Clearing House Committee made contact with all the known Family Groups. It also answered the

---

10. Now known as the AA General Service Office (GSO).

11. AA General Headquarters gave information to Lois W. (Al-Anon's co-founder and wife of Bill W.) about 87 groups and individuals.

inquiries that AA Headquarters had received from individuals. A survey showed that Family Groups bore a variety of names and that many versions of the Twelve Steps were in use. The group purposes were not always clear. A few groups were simply auxiliaries to AA groups—dispensers of coffee and cakes.

Other groups were meeting to learn how to get along with their alcoholic partners, with very little emphasis on the Twelve Steps as applied to themselves. But even those groups, which were forging ahead with high success, needed encouragement and contact with each other. Moreover, literature about Family Groups was non-existent.

After much correspondence and consultation, unity began to develop. The groups voted to adopt the name "The Al-Anon Family Groups" and they agreed that the Twelve Steps of Alcoholics Anonymous, virtually unchanged, should be the principles by which they would strive to conduct their lives. They authorized the Clearing House to handle overall public relations and the production of literature was begun.[12]

At this point the Family Group movement came to public attention. Magazine articles, in many cases prepared with the assistance of Clearing House members, drew a stream of inquiries. More volunteers rallied to the aid of the Clearing House Committee, as the influx of mail grew. New groups sprang up and began to write the Clearing House about their problems.

Family Groups soon appeared overseas[13]. By newsletters and mail, they were brought in contact with other groups throughout the world, and the Clearing House was able to direct travelers to them. The monthly newsletter was sent to lone members as well as groups, and with these isolated ones an encouraging personal correspondence was set up. A world directory was prepared and sent [to] all groups.[14] Additional literature was completed and more was projected.

12. See Appendix II, #3 re adoption of the Twelve Traditions.
13. In the 1950s, Al-Anon was present in Australia, Finland, New Zealand, South Africa, and the United Kingdom (UK) and Eire
14. In 1988 the World Service Conference voted to discontinue the printed world directory. Group information is available via toll-free phone lines.

By this time, in 1954, Clearing House activities had become strenuous. A new group was being born somewhere about every three days. Even though more members volunteered to meet this situation, a paid worker become a necessity.

[15]How is the Clearing House financed? From its very start the Al-Anon Family Groups have sent voluntary contributions, roughly determining the amounts by the formula, "one dollar for each member, Spring and Fall."[16] The Clearing House also has a small income[17] from the sale of literature, a list of which appears on page 96 of the Appendix.[18]

The Clearing House books are audited by a CPA, and regular financial reports are made to contributors.

In order to handle its essential business affairs and modest bank balance more efficiently, the original Clearing House committee is now incorporated as a non-profit unit known as The Al-Anon Family Group Headquarters, Inc.

Trustees[19] of the Al-Anon Headquarters are assisted by an Advisory Committee, usually volunteer members of the Clearing House. It is hoped that this committee can eventually develop into a yearly service conference[20] of delegates representing Family Groups everywhere, again following the pattern of growth and development of the structure of Alcoholics Anonymous.

---

15. In the second printing of the book, the order of the next four paragraphs was changed but the text was not altered, except where noted.

16. In 2000 the suggested donation is five dollars per member on a quarterly basis.

17. Income from contributions and the sale of literature has remained relatively stable in proportion to WSO operational expenses.

18. In the second printing the list was deleted, and the new statement was "a price list which may be obtained from Headquarters."

19. See Appendix II, # 4 for the definitions of regional trustees, trustees-at-large and Board of Trustees.

20. The first trial annual World Service Conference was held in 1961. In 1963 the Conference voted to make the World Service Conference permanent beginning in 1964.

The Family Groups And You[21]

Why should you be interested in the Al-Anon Family Groups?

Perhaps you are a non-alcoholic who has been hurt by the compulsive drinking of an alcoholic husband, wife or friend. Or perhaps you are married to an alcoholic who has already achieved sobriety, and you would now like to benefit from the experience of others like yourself who have reconstructed their personal and family relationships damaged through alcoholism.

In either case—whether you are concerned with your relationship to someone who is still drinking out of control, or to someone who has achieved sound sobriety—this handbook may be helpful to you.

You will note on the following pages that the emphasis in the Family Groups is not upon what can be done to, or with, the alcoholic in your life; it is upon what *you* can do with your own life. How can you make it happier and more effective, thus improving your partner's chances for permanent recovery?

Your answers to one or more of the following questions may determine whether or not the Family Groups can help you:

1. Are you the wife, husband, relative or friend of a problem drinker who still *refuses* help?

2. Are you concerned with a member of AA who is still having trouble with alcohol?

3. Though the alcoholic member of your family may now be sober, do you still feel that your home life is insecure or difficult?

4. Do you understand fully how alcoholism and its consequences may have warped your own thinking and your own personality?

---

21. In 1960 the chapter titled "Is Al-Anon for You?" was added to the book. In 1974, with the fifth printing of the revised expanded version, this chapter included pertinent excerpts from the 1960 revision. See Appendix II, #5.

5. Do you know that you can find understanding, friendship and help in the Al-Anon Family Groups, (a) regardless of whether the alcoholic member of your family has sobered up, or (b) whether he has made good in his business affairs, or (c) whether normal family relations have been restored?

6. Do you know that your own ability to face every life problem serenely and with a constructive attitude can be a most important factor in helping your alcoholic partner to achieve a full and happy recovery from problem drinking?

The men and women of the Al-Anon Family Groups have had to face all these questions. They have had to take stock and realize that their partner's alcoholism has often affected them, too. By learning from other Al-Anon members who have successfully dealt with these problems, they have been able to create far happier personal relations and much better home lives even under difficult conditions.

From the experience of thousands of these non-alcoholics have come certain principles and approaches that can be helpful to you.

Understanding The Alcoholic[22]

Knowledge and understanding in a family are the keys to build-ing a better life with an alcoholic. This means that it is important to understand the nature of alcoholism itself, a malady so little understood for centuries. Alcoholism has been a serious personal and social problem from the beginning of civilization. Doctors, spir-itual leaders, friends and relatives have always tried to help the alcoholic, with little real success until recent years.

Today, however, there is a new and promising approach, an increasing recognition of the fact that alcoholism is an illness and that the alcoholic is truly a sick person. One of the most exciting dis-coveries is that alcoholism *can* actually be checked, even if the illness itself cannot be cured. This parallels increasing knowledge in dealing with other health problems, notably diabetes. Although no cure for diabetes has ever been discovered, we now know that the diabetic can arrest his illness and live a normal life so long as he avoids sugar, continues to take insulin *and* follows a common sense diet.

[23]Our present knowledge that the alcoholic is a sick person means that we cannot expect to help him with his problem by blaming him for his lack of will power or pleading with him to con-sider the damage he is doing to himself, his family or his business prospects. We have learned that his drinking is now completely out of control and has become an obsession. Even though he originally may have brought his condition upon himself, he is now sick and to some extent not responsible. At this stage we cannot blame him for his illness any more than we would blame victims of other mal-adies. We do the best we can to help or to make help available.

Very often the non-alcoholic partner thinks that he or she is the real victim of alcoholism, perhaps even the cause. After years of liv-ing with a problem drinker, the non-alcoholic may feel that the alcoholic is rebelling against his partner and expressing his resent-

---

22. In 1960 four sub-headings were added, as noted. In March 1966 the title of this chapter was changed to "Understanding Alcoholism the Illness."

23. The sub-heading "Alcoholism is a Disease" was added in 1960.

ment through irresponsible drinking. The non-alcoholic may indeed have aggravated the condition. But the truth seems to be that the causes of alcoholism lie much deeper than this. Very often basic personality flaws can be traced back to the alcoholic's childhood. Therefore, partners of alcoholics should blame neither themselves nor the alcoholic.

[24] Are alcoholics apt to have any distinguishing personality traits?

A few *can* be recognized, although it should be remembered that not all alcoholics react in the same way.

Alcoholics are likely to be persons of intense, if brief, enthusiasms. They have a tendency to try to do too much too fast. They are apt to demand perfection in themselves and in others, too. When frustrated, they are likely to be over-depressed or over-aggressive. Hence, they often lack the emotional stability to face life's problems in a realistic manner.

Alcoholics are generally most attractive and intelligent people. They may hold very high ideals, which they seem unable to practice in daily living. Their attractive qualities account for the fact that so many non-alcoholics choose them as life partners.

When the alcoholic is drinking, his fine qualities disappear. At such times everything else is secondary to an irresistible craving for alcohol. His kindness, when he exhibits it, is often irrational. Many wives of alcoholics can recall sadly the times their husbands squandered small fortunes on flowers or lavish gifts while household bills went unnoticed and unpaid.

In many cases the alcoholic does not *want* to recover. This is because he rarely has clear insight into the serious nature of his illness and what must be done to cope with it. The alcoholic's thinking is often warped and distorted. In spite of every evidence, he may even refuse to admit that he is an alcoholic at all. He may reject the fact that once he has become an alcoholic, he can never drink normally again. This is a bitter pill for most problem drinkers. They

---

24. The sub-heading "The Alcoholic Personality" was added in 1960.

hope against hope that medical evidence is wrong, that their own case is somehow different and that in some mysterious way they will be able to keep their drinking under control.

All the medical evidence points to the opposite direction. To the best of medical knowledge, no one who has crossed the borderline from social to alcoholic drinking has ever been able to drink temperately again. And since alcoholism definitely appears to be a progressive illness, the situation over a period of time almost never gets better; it usually gets worse.[25]

[26]The alcoholic in your life may fit into one of four fairly common categories:

1. He may be a heavy drinker who has not been hurt too badly, or has not hurt others seriously. His drinking may be confined largely to weekends or special occasions and he may have lost little, if any, time from his job. The main disturbing factor may be that the periods between bouts are getting shorter and the drinking itself heavier. This person is probably just on the borderline of alcoholism. While he may be able to keep his drinking under control, he is probably on the way to becoming a full-fledged alcoholic.

2. Perhaps he is a drinker who is just beginning to have serious problems. He may have lost a job or two and his family life may have become tense and unhappy. He recognizes that he should "do something about his drinking" but refuses to consider the possibility of outside help. He thinks he can handle his problem alone. Meanwhile, his drinking continues to get worse, with increasing damage to his home and business life.

3. In the third stage of progressive drinking, the alcoholic himself recognizes that drinking is a problem that he cannot control. By this time, there is ample evidence. His family relationships may have been badly shattered. He may have been jailed for brief periods as a result of drunken escapades. He may

---

25. "...until radical steps are taken to arrest the progression" was added in 1966.
26. In 1960 the sub-heading "Alcoholic Patterns" was added.

have lost a succession of jobs. At this point, the alcoholic often wavers between a sincere desire to quit drinking (usually following a particularly bad spree) and a stubborn resistance to help.

4. In the most serious stage of alcoholism, the problem drinker seems completely "lost" and beyond hope of recovery. Probably he has been hospitalized or committed to special institutions. He has drifted away from all normal sense of responsibility, perhaps forsaking family, friends and every other aspect of normal living, and if no one protects him, he may land on some skid row.[27]

For permanent sobriety, the one absolute imperative is that the alcoholic must desire deeply and sincerely to stop drinking for the rest of his life.[28]

Two facts deserve emphasis. The first is that few alcoholics, including those who have reached the fourth stage described above, can be said to be beyond hope. So long as the alcoholic retains the ability really to understand what his malady is and that he can do something about it, there is much reason to hope for his recovery, based on the experience of those now sober in AA.

The second fact is that alcoholism does not respect sex. Both men and women can be found in the various categories outlined above. Many men will recognize a loved one in the drinking patterns already described. The consequences of a woman's irrational drinking may be hidden longer than that of a man. But the grave and progressive nature of the illness is common to both.

Your understanding of alcoholism and of the alcoholic is incomplete unless you recognize the limitations that confront the non-alcoholic in dealing with the problem. Pleading, cajoling, pampering and scolding are never effective in getting the alcoholic to quit drinking. As members of AA phrase it, the alcoholic usually has to

---

27. In 1966 a fifth stage was added: "5. Beyond this lies insanity or death."
28. In 1960 the sub-heading "Prelude to Sobriety" was added.

"hit bottom" for himself or herself before an effective decision to stop drinking can be made.

The alcoholic may hit a mental, emotional or physical bottom— or indeed all three. This means that he is ready to admit defeat— that he cannot cope with this problem alone.

Not all alcoholics "hit bottom" at the same stage of their drinking. Some recognize early that they are on the way to possible disaster. Seeing the inevitable catastrophe ahead, they turn to AA or perhaps to other sources for help.

Other alcoholics are not so fortunate. They have to go farther down the scale in their drinking before they are able to admit that they cannot control alcohol and that they must have outside help.

This situation is most difficult for the non-alcoholic. Wanting to be helpful, eager to build a constructive life for the loved one, the non-alcoholic partner is obliged to patiently wait until the problem drinker himself can face up to his problem. Nevertheless, in the meantime, there is much that the non-alcoholic can do. A change in her attitude may hasten his decision.

The experience of the Al-Anon Family Groups certainly proves that it is never too late—nor too early—to try to understand ourselves, as non-alcoholic, in relation to the alcoholic.

Understanding Ourselves[29]

While our alcoholic partners were still drinking, and before we knew anything about alcoholism, we were acutely sensitive to the hurt they caused us. In the privacy of our own thoughts—sometimes not too privately—we had a number of ways of describing the men and women who alternately seemed so dear and so strange to us.

We oftentimes said they were selfish, arrogant, irresponsible and lacking in appreciation of us. We reproached them for the time they spent away from home. We accused them of failing in their duties and privileges as partners, fathers, mothers, or children. We railed at them for their failure to handle money wisely and their unconcern for the future. Humanly speaking, there was usually plenty of justification for these attitudes. Our blame of them was natural for we did not know that our partners were very sick people.

Often enough, we wrapped a mantle of complete self-righteousness about our own thoughts and actions. Occasionally, in desperation and bitterness, we tried to retaliate in various ways. Sometimes we even got drunk ourselves.

But after our partners joined Alcoholics Anonymous and we ourselves attended open meetings, we began to benefit greatly. We noted, first of all, that the AA program usually resulted in a profound change in the thinking and everyday behavior of sober alcoholics. This change, affecting the entire personality of the alcoholic, seemed to come about as a result of an honest and searching personal inventory of his own faults.

Another thing we especially noticed was that when we non-alcoholics began to talk with one another and exchange ideas, we frequently were able to apply another's experience to our own particular problems.

As non-alcoholic partners, we discovered we had as much to gain through AA's "Suggested Twelve Steps of Recovery" as the alcoholics did. We found that alcoholism had made us sick, too. We

---

29. In 1960 the sub-heading "Before Sobriety" was added.

needed emotional sobriety as much as the alcoholic needed freedom from alcohol. When we began to examine our own attitudes,
many of us were amazed to see how twisted and warped much of our
thinking had become.

We sometimes found that a great many of our attitudes had
become negative. We were often mired in cynicism and despair.
Some of us had lost faith in the goodness of life and so had lost faith
in ourselves. Many of us dared not hope that the miracle of sobriety could be granted to our alcoholic spouse. Often, in our deep dis-
content, we were too apathetic to believe in the possibility of a
change. Even those of us who tried to cling to the spiritual
resources of our youth often did so without firm conviction or positive expectation.

Clearly, these cobwebs of cynicism and despair had to be brushed
out of our thinking before we could make a new and successful
approach to the problem of living with an alcoholic—whether
drinking or not.

Many of us also discovered, when we looked inward, that unconsciously we had been developing a marked arrogance. Because our
alcoholic partners had been so patently "wrong," we tended to
assume that we were infallibly "right" in most of our attitudes and
decisions. Moreover, our friends and sympathetic public opinion
encouraged this. Our sense of rightness and authority over our alcoholic partners appeared in many matters, great and small.
Unknowingly, we had become the parents of wayward children.
What we intended as loving direction often turned into thoughtless
domination and nagging.

We were frequently overwhelmed by self-pity. Life, we thought,
had been cruel in saddling us with an alcoholic partner. Often
enough we concentrated too much on this one fact. We forgot that
our alcoholic mate could have been the kindest and most generous
person in the world when sober. Maybe we had been blessed with

good health and fine children. We forgot that, too. Perhaps we still enjoyed our certain amount of material prosperity due entirely to the industry and ambition of the alcoholic in his sober periods. He had often tried his best to make things pleasant for us. We often forgot to count our blessings; we harped too much upon our burdens.

[30]When husbands were drinking out of control, we wives frequently had to assume extra family responsibilities, often becoming breadwinners and, in many cases, heads of the household. Because our partners were unpredictable, we were forced into the habit of making all the main decisions ourselves. When our partners sobered up in AA and became qualified to assume responsibility, we were not always willing to let them do so. Running things our own way had become a deeply ingrained habit. So when alcoholics tried to resume partnership responsibilities, they often met resistance from us and tensions developed, which might have been avoided through an Easy Does It attitude.

Of course, not all of us were guilty of all these negative habits. We did not all become shrews, or lose hope completely or seek avenues of revenge and escape. Many of the unpleasant things about ourselves lay deep below the surface. For example, when our partners first joined AA and underwent a miraculous change, life seemed to most of us very rosy indeed. What we had hoped and striven for all through the years had now become a reality. For a few of us this bright prospect never dimmed, but for most of us that was not the case.

For some reason life simply would not stay rosy. We still felt vaguely insecure. We lacked serenity for today and the confidence for tomorrow. We quarreled with the alcoholic over trifles. We found that the process of adjusting to our partner's new way of life in AA brought a fresh set of problems—problems which we must solve of ourselves and in ourselves if a happy home life was to be recreated. We saw how much we, too, could benefit by living

---

30. In 1960 the sub-heading "After Sobriety" was added. Additionally, there were substantial revisions to the following paragraphs. See Appendix II, #6.

according to AA's Twelve Steps, applying these principles to our own lives.

Little by little we became more honest with ourselves. Some of us began to realize, for example, that many of our defects had no relation to our partner's alcoholism, perhaps having developed in childhood. Our experience with alcoholism had only hardened them. Or maybe we recognized that we still harbored resentments, unconsciously rebelling against the burden of the past. Perhaps we resented the fact that someone other than ourselves had been able to help our partner to stop drinking. Some of us resented the time that the sober alcoholic now spent at AA meetings, or in working with alcoholics who were still drinking. We were not immune to resentments over the fact that a newly-sober husband now labored long and diligently to make up for lost time in his business affairs. In time we came to realize this was possessiveness and not true partnership.

Even though we had learned to release our partners to their AA activities and their business lives, some of us still felt isolated and lonely. We knew that the alcoholic, even if he had family ties, felt himself to be the loneliest person in the world before he found Alcoholics Anonymous. That was a clue to the way out of our own personal dilemma of loneliness. We saw that the recovered alcoholic eased his burdens by sharing his experiences with others who understood him. Since this sharing benefited alcoholics, might it not be helpful for their non-alcoholic partners as well? In the Al-Anon Family Groups we do just that and find our answer.

The Family Group Program At Work[31]

The family group program charts a new way of life for the non-alcoholic, just as AA is a new approach to living for the problem drinker. How does the Family Group program work? What are is basic principles? How can they be applied to daily living? And if AA in open meetings is already available to partners, why do we need Family Groups?

Let's take the last question first. Some of us who had gone to open AA meetings had applied the Steps more or less vaguely to ourselves. But we had not realized that in working the program thoroughly and in company with others with like needs, we could thus derive so much additional benefit ourselves. We do not only help each other; we also form warm and fast friendships from such close association. Any AA will say that his most rewarding activity is that of carrying the message to the alcoholic who still suffers, whether by personal sponsorship or in closed meetings. Al-Anon groups give us the exact equivalent of this important Twelfth Step work. They enable us to bring our unique experience and understanding as non-alcoholic partners to wives, husbands, relatives and friends of alcoholics who seek our aid.

As to the other questions, members of Family Groups base their lives squarely upon the Twelve Steps of Alcoholics Anonymous. Although these steps were originally designed for alcoholics, it has been found that they offer a solution for most of the problems of daily living. These are the Twelve Steps[32]:

1. We admitted we were powerless over alcohol—that our lives had become unmanageable.

---

31. In 1960 this chapter was replaced with a chapter on the Twelve Steps Appendix II, #7), and a chapter on the Twelve Traditions (Appendix II, #8) was added. A new chapter, titled "Al-Anon and the Family" (Appendix II, #9) consolidated portions of the "The Family Group Program at Work" with the original chapters titled "The Sex Problem" and "Do Husbands of Alcoholics Need Family Groups, Too?" In 1974 new text was added to this chapter. With the September 1976 printing the sub-title "Al-Anon Is for Women" was added (Appendix II, #10).

32. of AA

2. Came to believe that a Power greater than ourselves could restore us to sanity.

3. Made a decision to turn our will and our lives over to the care of God *as we understood Him.*

4. Made a searching and fearless moral inventory of ourselves.

5. Admitted to God, to ourselves, and to another human being the exact nature of our wrongs.

6. Were entirely ready to have God remove all these defects of character.

7. Humbly asked Him to remove our shortcomings.

8. Made a list of all persons we had harmed, and became willing to make amends to them all.

9. Made direct amends to such people wherever possible, except when to do so would injure them or others.

10. Continued to take personal inventory and when we were wrong promptly admitted it.

11. Sought through prayer and meditation to improve our conscious contact with God, *as we understood Him,* praying only for knowledge of His will for us, and the power to carry that out.

12. Having had a spiritual awakening as the result of these Steps, we tried to carry this message to alcoholics, and to practice these principles in all our affairs.

The only change necessary to make these AA Steps completely applicable to ourselves is the substitution of "others" for the word "alcoholics" in the last Step. Notice that even the phrase, "We admitted we were powerless over alcohol," is appropriate to the partner of the alcoholic, too. For certainly we non-alcoholics were powerless to help our husbands, wives or friends to control alcohol. To us, as to them, alcohol was an overpowering problem.

Of course, nearly all of us were inspired by the beauty and power of the Twelve Steps as they affected our partners. But some of us, having the mistaken feeling that we had always lived by similar principles, could not see the need for their application to ourselves. To others the Steps seemed to be a prescription for perfection. We doubted that we could follow them literally. We were not even sure that we were ready to follow them at all.

Members with greater experience in the Family Group program were quick to reassure us. The Twelve Steps are guides to a new life, we were told; they are not rigid requirements. Very few people try to do all of them at once. The usefulness of the Steps, our friend said, has been proved through experience; they are not theoretical. By constantly holding them in mind, and trying to follow them to the best of our ability, our thinking and actions are directed into positive, constructive channels. Little by little, we make progress, one step at a time. The main thing is that we go on trying.

We found that Step One—the admission that we needed help and that we could not handle the job alone—was tremendously effective. Wonderfully, this lifted a burden from us and relieved our crushing feeling of inadequacy. It led to a new, radical concept of our basic responsibility to the alcoholic we loved and wanted to help.

We suddenly saw that we had been trying to do the impossible. Attempting to manage, control, doctor or pamper the alcoholic led nowhere. We then realized we must try to understand both the nature of his illness and its effect upon us. This greatly relieved the guilt and blame with which we had both been plagued. But, above all, we non-alcoholics found we had to let go of the problem. Literally, we had to Let Go and Let God.

It is not always easy for us to "get out of the driver's seat" and to admit our lack of personal power to cure alcoholism. The habits of belief and action of many years' duration are hard to overcome. But when we saw that the Family Group approach had worked for others, we became willing to try it.

We soon saw that all of the Twelve Steps are very important indeed. But certain ones are not only important but indispensable if any progress is to be made. This is particularly true of Steps Four and Ten—"Made a fearless moral inventory" and "Continued to take personal inventory and when we were wrong promptly admitted it." To make these steps really effective we found we had to clinch them with Step Five—"Admitted to God, to ourselves and to *another human being* the exact nature of our wrongs." These Steps involve, of course, the very healthy practice of non-morbid self-analysis of one's own defects and of a discussion of them with another person. Religion, psychiatry, AA and the Al-Anon Family Groups, all four, are unanimous in their opinion that little emotional or spiritual growth is possible unless these principles of self-searching are continually practiced.

An inventory includes personal assets as well as liabilities. It is important that we look at both in order to have a reasonable and balanced picture of ourselves. We who have lived with alcoholics have tried to do our best. In most cases, we have not lacked courage, loyalty, perseverance or love as we then understood these things.

But now comes a vital question. Possessing all these positive virtues, did we not also have many serious defects, conscious or unconscious? Asked this question the average newcomer to our groups usually says: "No, I really don't believe so. I have lived a good life and have done the best I could."

Here is the point at which we can help. For each of us, even the best of us, has found that alcoholism terribly aggravated our natural defects. What made it hard to take our inventory and see these defects was the fact that most of them seemed justified. After all, weren't we entitled to be depressed one day and dominating the

next? Who would run things if we didn't? Why shouldn't we crave
sympathy or feel self-pity? What if we did hound the alcoholic to go
out and make a living? Suppose we did retaliate a little sometimes?
Who could blame us or why should we blame ourselves?

We of the Family Groups have found that blame of ourselves or
others solves no problems. The real question is whether we still
carry any of these ground-in habit patterns and destructive attitudes
into our present day lives. A careful self-examination, usually at
first aided by a more experienced member, invariably shows a surprising "hangover" of these old-time liabilities. But many of them
may not be obvious to us in the beginning. Irritation over trifles
may be covering up repressed resentment and anger. The insistence
on running everything, on petty nagging and bossing, we justified
as helping the alcoholic. Over-possessiveness of our partners may
have developed because of hidden jealousy of AA or the world outside.

When we continue to look hard and willingly, we discover more
and more harmful characteristics. And we also see that the subtle
and hidden defects can be as bad as the obvious ones. Indeed, sometimes they are worse because they are so hard to root out and cast
away.

For most of us the attempt at such a thorough self-examination,
first alone and then with another person, was not a bit easy. After
years of living with a problem drinker, most of us retreated to a
lonely little world of our own. Many of us were shy by nature. Years
of suffering the effects of alcoholism, of having our words resented
and misunderstood, did little to encourage us to talk things out with
anyone. When we finally decided to discuss our problems, we still
held back certain painful experiences. These, we thought, would
have to go to our graves with us. But when we made it our business
to select a person in whom we could safely and fully confide—perhaps a Family Group member, a doctor, or a spiritual advisor—the

relief was immense. We were no longer afraid or alone. From this point on we found it much easier to discuss problems with our partners and children at home. We could talk in terms of hope, rather than in the bitter language of recrimination. We could stress the important things we had in common, rather than the petty things that divided us.

We tried not to bottle up resentments or let them fester inside. We tried to face each problem and irritation as it arose, to clear it out of the atmosphere and thus free ourselves for daily tasks. We tried to act and think in terms of what we could accomplish today, rather than dream grandiosely of what might happen in the distant future. Surprisingly, we found we could confess our own faults freely whenever that seemed right, helpful or prudent. And, most important, we stopped harping on our partner's faults. We and our families began to experience peace of mind.

Members who had been in the group a long time and whose husbands perhaps had been happy in AA many years, encouraged us by the very fact of their presence at the meetings and their responsibility and interest in passing on the help they themselves had received.

We asked questions and sought explanations from these members. And, in turn, we encouraged other newcomers to share their problems with us when we could be helpful.

Thus we learned the value of continuous self-examination and a ready willingness to admit mistakes.

Many of us were confused by the suggestion that we make amends to all persons we had harmed. To us, as partners of alcoholics, it had always seemed that amends were due us, rather than the other way around. When, however, we began to examine our attitudes and actions objectively, it became much clearer that this business of making amends is nearly always a two-way proposition.

Deliberately or otherwise, nearly all of us had done and said things that we now had occasion to regret.

We learned that *willingness* to make amends was the important thing. In a few cases, of course, it might be unwise to open old wounds but generally, we were told, thoroughness was really necessary—prudence and good timing being understood. It usually takes much willingness to offer reparation for the mistakes of the past. But when that condition is fulfilled, the dividends are great. When we examined ourselves, we cleaned house inside; now we clear away the debris of the past on the outside by mending strained or broken relationships with those about us.

When we looked at Family Group members who had achieved serenity and a new way of life, we found that they all practiced meditation and prayer. To most of us this was no new idea, for we had meditated long and often in the past; we had certainly prayed for deliverance from the burden alcoholism had imposed upon us. But our meditations and prayers could be improved; they often had been little more than brooding and demanding.

From the Family Groups we learned to look both inward and upward. Our inward searching was designed to remove pettiness and self-pity from our mind and soul. Our upward searching was a new attempt to bring our thinking in harmony with the finest and highest ideals we knew—either as the result of religious observance, the Twelve Steps, or other inspirational channels.

When we prayed, it was no longer for specific miracles or tangible material benefits. We prayed for knowledge and understanding that would guide us in daily actions. And we prayed for the courage and power to act in accordance with that knowledge and understanding. We centered our prayers on finding God's will for us, whatever that might be. Therefore, the words of the "AA prayer"[33] became very important to us:

---

33. The Serenity Prayer was formerly called The AA Prayer.

"God grant me the serenity to accept the things I cannot change, the courage to change the things I can, and the wisdom to know the difference."[34]

This was different from the kind of praying many of us had done in the past. We no longer asked God to change our spouse's drinking habits overnight, or to restore our finances or to make our lives easier. Instead, we sought guidance and strength to enable us to work out our own problems.

The Family Group program is essentially a program of spiritual growth. It is not a religious program, if by "religious" we mean creed or ritual. But it does emphasize the peace and harmony that can be attained by living in accordance with spiritual principles common to all religions. Of first importance is the principle that we can gain needed strength for daily living by placing complete reliance upon a Higher Power.

Most men and women call their Higher Power God. But to make room for all, the Family Groups carefully leave the naming of "the Higher Power" to each individual. They know that everyone may not be prepared or ready to accept God by name. In seeking to grow spiritually, the Family Group member tries to increase his or her awareness of a Greater or Higher Power which can be relied upon for help. It is an interesting fact that even agnostic members finally begin to name their Higher Power "God."

To help others is to help ourselves. When Family Group members help the distraught relatives of alcoholics as only they can, they themselves make great gains in emotional stability and spiritual progress. They shed their own problems by becoming interested in the problems of others.

This activity is perhaps the primary reason for the existence of our Al-Anon Family Groups and it centers around the Twelfth Step of our program, which reads as follows:

---

34. Appendix II, #2.

"Having had a spiritual awakening as a result of these steps, we tried to carry the[35] message to others and practice these principles in all our affairs."

Two key thoughts are conveyed by this Step. The first is the importance of carrying the message to others. The second is the importance of practicing all Twelve Steps in daily living.

The message of the Family Groups is a story of proved results. Because of their wide and varied experience, Family Group members are able to help in many directions. When the alcoholic partner is already in AA and making fine progress, they can help members of his family develop happier homes. Where the alcoholic, though in AA, is still emotionally unstable or barely sober, Family Group members can be singularly helpful. They can bring comfort, counsel and help as none other can. Even more is this true when the Family Group members share their experience with the wives or relatives of alcoholics who are still drinking and not yet ready for AA. They can show how a sane and useful life is possible even with a drinking partner. The realization that these partners are sick, and the change in attitude that follows this realization, frequently helps the problem drinkers themselves to join AA months or years earlier than they otherwise would.

This is only a partial accounting of the benefits which any partner or relative of an alcoholic may find by practicing the Twelve Steps as a new way of life in the Al-Anon Family Groups. The almost invariable results are a far brighter home life, a much finer relation with everyone, the building of warm friendships and the lessening of fear and loneliness. For those who must still carry heavy burdens, the new-found ability to face problems with firmness, faith and hope is priceless.

---

35. In the original text the word "the" was used rather than "this," which is the correct wording of the Twelfth Step.

The Sex Problem

Among the many problems that living with an alcoholic presents is that of the sex relations.

It is rare indeed for a married couple to have a normal sex life while alcoholism is active. And even after the alcoholic has sobered up, considerable difficulty may persist.

Because drinking usually breaks down inhibitions, almost anything can happen to a tipsy man or woman. And it often does. On the other hand, some alcoholics drink until they are so sodden and their senses so dulled that nothing but more liquor interests them.

In either case, no mate can be attracted to a drunken wife or husband. Many a wife is filled with repugnance and even terror at the approach of her intoxicated partner. She often feels as though the marriage relation was being prostituted. Not infrequently a mate, finding husband or wife drunk at home, has revolted and sought an alliance elsewhere.

When such complications have been serious, it is not surprising that they sometimes persist after the alcoholic has achieved sobriety.

Though we cannot here cover all the ramifications of the sex problem, we in the Family Groups have had actual experience in practically every phase of this difficulty. And, fortunately, most of us so afflicted have found workable solutions for the larger share of these troubles.[36] This is happily demonstrated by the very low divorce rate among well established AA couples.

Therefore, we strongly urge every newcomer who lives with a disturbing problem of this kind to carefully choose a member of the Family Group for counsel and comfort. A free discussion with such a person in strict confidence will invariably bring great relief and encouragement.

---

36. This sentence was deleted in the January 1976 edition.

For further study of this problem, and the other psychological effects of living with an alcoholic, there is a helpful pamphlet, "The Alcoholic's Wife—Her Problems," written by the secretary of a Family Group.[37]

Affiliation with the Family Groups certainly offers no cure-all for the complex problems of marriage and sex as they are affected by alcoholism.[38] But the success that has been achieved by Family Group members has been encouraging; it can be the basis for real hope for every newcomer.

---

37. This publication is no longer available.

38. The second printing added: "and in several cases it is of course wise to seek the advice also of a doctor, minister or marriage counselor."

Do Husbands of Alcoholics Need Family Groups, Too?[39]

Husbands of alcoholic women and fathers of alcoholic children play an important role in the Al-Anon Family Groups. Although they are in the minority, because male alcoholics far outnumber female, they find that the Al-Anon experience and way of life can be a solvent for their problems, too.

Notwithstanding economic and psychological differences distinguishing the situations of wives of alcoholics from husbands of alcoholic, it has been found that Family Groups can be equally helpful to both. The husband of a woman addict can feel just as helpless and hopeless as any wife of a problem drinker; his lack of understanding of alcoholism, and what to do about it, can be quite as abysmal as hers.

All partners of alcoholics, whether women or men, find that they have a great deal in common. But in some respects the home of a woman drinker does present special problems.

The wife of an alcoholic often feels she must hold the home together for economic reasons or for the sake of the children. These reasons do not affect the husband of a problem drinker so strongly. The man is the normal breadwinner and financially free to go or stay. Hence marriages where the woman is alcoholic tend to break up sooner. Indeed most of the early AA women had lost their husbands before AA came into their lives.

But when the husband of an alcoholic woman does stand by until she joins AA, the problem of readjustment is less severe. The non-alcoholic man has been head of the house all along. Therefore there is not the usual bad warp in the marriage relation caused by the wife of the alcoholic having to assume the responsibilities of breadwinning. True, many husbands of alcoholic women do become altogether too fatherly and too possessive. Nevertheless, it

---

39. The title which appears in the table of contents is, "Do Husbands of Alcoholics Need the Family Groups?"

is usually easier for them to stop treating their wives as erring children.

The fact that men are apt to be less patient and steadfast than women poses another difficulty. Men are more easily discouraged and quicker to give up if their wives do not respond promptly to AA They are likely to expect too much, too soon, and their patience often fails when their partners, though sober, continue to be temperamental and hard to live with.

Then, too, the stigma of drinking falls more heavily upon women and their husbands are apt to feel this most keenly, reacting in deep resentment and sometimes with actual contempt. A conscious or unconscious hangover of these feelings makes full reconciliation and partnership difficult, even though the wife is doing well in AA.

Previously there was little for grieved and frustrated husbands to do except to take leave of their alcoholic wives. But today with the help of Al-Anon Groups, many a husband is holding together a home which otherwise would have fallen apart. Family Group meetings often include several husbands or fathers of alcoholics. We know of one group composed principally of male relatives of problem drinkers.[40]

Because AA is now much better known and reaches younger people, women alcoholics are coming into AA earlier in their drinking careers. Many AA women still have their husbands, who often join Family Groups. And more husbands are attending Family Group meetings, whether their wives have joined AA or not. They are grateful to learn that their alcoholic wives are really sick, that patience and love and understanding on their part can do much towards aiding their partners' recovery.

Therefore, husbands as well as other male relatives of alcoholics can find real answers to their problems in Al-Anon Family Groups. To all such seekers we open our doors in special welcome.

---

40. See Who Are the Members of Al-Anon/Alateen? (S-29) for current statistics.

Children Of Alcoholics[41]

How to protect children in the home of an alcoholic is a problem very close to the heart of every Family Group parent. In spite
of all that can be done, children of active alcoholics usually become
aware that there is something seriously wrong in their home, making it very different from the homes of their playmates.
Consequently, many of these young folks have been more or less
emotionally hurt. Though we cannot here discuss all these damages
in detail, we can suggest remedies for most of them.

When parents practice AA principles, the children always benefit. Indeed, the changes so wrought in youngsters sometimes pass all
expectation. Willing obedience takes the place of defiance, pride in
their parents replaces shame, the feeling of being alone and
unwanted disappears, and resentment changes to love.

The questions of when and how to let the children know that
their parent is an alcoholic or a member of AA are, of course, practical matters for the family to decide. But youngsters take in far
more than we realize. Many families have had remarkably good
results by explaining to even young children that their father has
been a sick man, that the disagreeable things he sometimes said and
did were the results of his illness, that their real father always wanted to be kind and loving.

Other children sometimes say cruel things to the children of
alcoholics, such as "My dad is better than yours. He never gets
drunk the way your old man does." A great deal of the sting is taken
out of such remarks if the mother has already explained to the child
that the father, whether in AA or not, is not bad but ill, and that
some day he will get well and become as fine a parent as anyone
ever had.

---

41. This chapter was condensed to a couple of paragraphs when the Alateen
    Chapter was added (See Appendix II, #11 and #12.) Alateen was formed in
    1957, two years after this book was first published.

Knowledge of AA makes most young people proud of their fathers. They like to be told about the positive, constructive things in AA, about the Twelve Steps and how their parents are trying to live by them, how, by helping others to recover, their father is also helping himself. The Steps appeal to the idealism of youth, and young folks will often want to be part of their family team in working with the Steps. It is so much easier for the family when the children know why their father is bringing home so many assorted people and why he has to go out so often, sometimes very suddenly, on Twelfth Step cases.

To help the young people understand AA better, many parents take them to selected open meetings. And, of course, Family Groups always welcome young folks. Some Al-Anon Groups hold special meetings in which the young are the principal speakers.

At times, children have been the means of their parents joining AA. There is a moving story about Johnny, a youngster who became very enthusiastic about AA after his dad joined. One day at school a temperance worker gave his class a lecture on the evils of drinking. Johnny was indignant when she labeled alcoholics as wicked. After the temperance worker left, he stood up and told his class that Alcoholics Anonymous taught that the alcoholic was a sick person who could get well through practicing AA's Twelve Steps. And, continued Johnny, if any of the class were having such trouble at home he would tell them after school where they could find help. One boy did appeal to Johnny and, as a result, this boy's father found sobriety in AA.

In another case an, AA member's daughter had a heart-to-heart talk about alcoholism with her roommate at college. The roommate realized that her own mother was an alcoholic. Returning home at vacation time, she explained the AA approach to alcoholism and, as a result, her mother soon joined AA, too.

The situations of children of alcoholic mothers, before the latter become AAs, are often complicated because fathers are not usually home in the daytime to protect them. But even so, an explanation that mother is ill and needs loving help will often make children feel useful and needed rather than hurt and unwanted. After joining AA, the alcoholic mother can explain these matters herself, thus enlisting the help of her children. A closer bond than ever before may well be the result.

Great patience on the part of parents is sometimes needed to restore their children's happiness. This is especially true where adolescent youth has been deeply hurt. Lacking a normal home life, such young people feel insecure and are filled with fear and resentment. They may sometimes make little response for months or even years, if the emotional damage is severe. But invariably the new way of life wins out. By avoiding overpersuasion, by confessing their own faults, but not demanding too much, and by persistently offering love, practically all AA and Family Group parents can, in time, correct the disturbing effect upon their children of living with an alcoholic.

What You Can Do[42]

If you are the partner, relative or friend of an alcoholic, we are confident the Family Group program can be helpful to you personally. Perhaps you wish to become affiliated with a Group in your own community.

The Al-Anon Family Group Headquarters (Post Office Box 1475, New York 17, NY)[43] can tell you if such a group is already in existence near your home. Or perhaps you can get such information by telephone from an AA member in your community.

But what if there is no Family Group near you? Many who are now members of active groups were once in the same position. Their answer was to take the initiative and start a group themselves. Nearly all groups have sprung from one person's need and desire for help from those who could share his or her experience.

The Clearing House will gladly provide you with any information that has not been covered in this booklet. It will reply to specific questions that may arise from time to time, utilizing the experience of the hundreds of groups already established. It will furnish names and addresses of other groups not too far from your community.

Many groups get under way with two or three persons meeting in each other's homes.

As the group becomes larger, the meeting may be moved to a convenient location in a church, school, library or some other semi-public building. Some groups find it desirable to meet in the same building utilized for AA closed meetings, with the two groups coming together for coffee after the separate meetings are concluded.

---

42. In 1960 this chapter was deleted, combined with the next chapter and titled "How to Find or Start a Group." The chapter was subsequently rewritten and expanded in future editions.

43. The current address of Al-Anon Family Group Headquarters, Inc. is 1600 Corporate Landing Parkway, Virginia Beach, VA 23454-5617.

In case you cannot form a group and hence must remain a lone member, you will find the Clearing House service invaluable. The staff there will be glad to maintain a correspondence with you, suggesting how you can apply what has been said in this booklet[44] to your own particular situation. You will also find in the Appendix a list of AA and Al-Anon publications which can be of great help.[45]

---

44. "Booklet" was changed to "volume" in the second printing.

45. The last sentence was changed in the second printing to read: "Besides this book, Headquarters publishes a number of helpful pamphlets on various phases of the work and a monthly periodical, The Family Group Forum." (Now known as The Forum.)

How To Start a Group

AL-ANON FAMILY GROUPS are started in two ways: (a) by a new group splitting off from an older group, or (b) by one or more individuals who, having heard about Al-Anon through publicity or personal contact, wish to start a group in their area.

When groups become unwieldy because of size (twenty is a workable membership) they sometimes divide for convenience. Again when members live at a distance from the established group they may want to have a group in their own community.

It is easy for the members of an established unit to form a new group because they know how a Family Group works. Also, the older group will always give them as much help as possible, going to their meetings, supplying speakers, and encouraging them in every way.

But others may have no experience to aid them, so it is for them particularly that the following paragraphs are written.

The Al-Anon Family Groups Headquarters will, of course, do all it can, including sending literature, or giving the location of any AA or Al-Anon group that may be near.[46]

If there is one of these groups in your vicinity, the first thing to do is to go to as many meetings as you can to absorb the fundamental ideas of AA and the Al-Anon Family Groups. At an AA meeting, talk to the wives and husbands of the members. You will probably find some kindred souls who will be anxious to help you form a Family Group.

By all means enlist the aid of AA members in your new project, explaining to them just how a Family Group will help AA as well as its own members. In most places, AA has been most cooperative, calling on Al-Anon to help the mates of new AA prospects, and announcing Al-Anon meetings when they make their own announcements. If AAs are not consulted and do not understand

---

46. Please call 1-888 4AL-ANON (1-888-425-2666) for assistance or check your local telephone directory.

the nature of your plans, they may naturally fear the breaking of their anonymity and so object to the activities of your group.

Of course, if there is a Family Group within easy traveling distance, your troubles are practically over, because as was said above, every older group is always glad to assist a new group.

In any case, tell your plans to your minister, your doctor, and any welfare agency you think would be helpful. These humanitarians will probably know some desperate wife or husband of an alcoholic who badly needs the help of a Family Group and who, if there is no group near you, may be an enthusiastic aid in starting one.

Besides bringing in members, these neighborhood friends can probably suggest a suitable inexpensive meeting place when you are ready for it.

One way to get new members is to put a small dignified announcement of the existence of such a group, giving time and place of meeting, in the local paper, being sure never to mention any names or in any way break an AA's anonymity. A PO Box number is a good camouflage.

Two or three members are sufficient to start a group. The atmosphere of a home is sociable and friendly and suitable for small meetings. But several groups have found that as the group grows, strangers will more readily go to a public meeting place than to a private home.

Do not be discouraged about the growth of your group. Most groups fluctuate greatly in attendance from time to time. Often the early enthusiasm of some of the members dwindles off. Al-Anon, like AA, is for those who really need it, and those who just come to warm their hands at its glow drop away. Then there are those who think they have received all that Al-Anon has to give, forgetting that we only really keep that which we pass on to others. If your group has helped ease the heartache and set on a path of growth only two or three members, it has been and is worthwhile.

Do not be afraid to start a group. Many others have done it. You, too, can do it. Besides, you will have the help of many friends, both at the Clearing House and in local groups. Groups near you will be glad to help personally; those at a distance, by correspondence.

After you have succeeded in getting a group running, do not be discouraged by the many ups and downs that are sure to come with growth. When difficulties arise, write the Clearing House. Probably some other group has gone through the same experience and we can report to you how that group weathered the storm. All experience can be made to serve a useful end. So all good wishes in your new venture.

Family Group Meetings and Procedure[47]

There is no rigid pattern for meetings. If the group is very small, a round table discussion is usually a practical way to handle a meeting. Experience suggests, however, that even the most informal sessions should have one central theme as a starting point. Discussion of one of the Twelve Steps, or one of the AA[48] slogans, can make a successful meeting.

As the group becomes larger, it may be well to follow the general pattern of AA meetings, with a "leader" to open and close and introduce two or three members who interpret their own experience in the Family Group. It is also desirable to have neighboring groups provide speakers on an exchange basis where possible.

Meetings usually open with a few moments of silence or "quiet time," and a welcome to newcomers. Many groups include the reading of the Twelve Steps, preceded by the Preamble, which you will find in the Appendix. Some groups include the reading and interpretation of[49] inspirational literature. Meetings conclude with the recital of the Lord's Prayer by all who care to share this tradition.[50]

Occasionally doctors or members of the clergy are asked to join with a group to contribute their viewpoints and experience on the subject of alcoholism in family life.[51]

Sometimes a member invites his alcoholic partner to speak on the same program, illustrating how their home life was straightened out.

In every meeting, the emphasis is on the principles of spiritual growth. We avoid critical references to alcoholic partners, or the recital of gossip or overly intimate personal details. The opportuni-

---

47. In 1960 this chapter was retitled "Al-Anon Meetings and Procedures." In later editions the chapter was moved near the back of the book.

48. Al-Anon

49. Al-Anon

50. See Appendix II, #19 for current suggested closing.

51. See *Al-Anon/Alateen Service Manual*, Policy Digest section, regarding Outside Speakers.

ty for full discussion is, of course, always provided in confidential conversations. Special efforts are made to welcome newcomers, to help them to feel at home, and to assist them in developing a new and healthy approach to life.

There is, naturally, no "formula" for a Family Group meeting talk. Most speakers begin by identifying themselves as the partner or relative of an alcoholic. They may suggest, in general terms, how life with an alcoholic affected them. They may outline various attempts they made to cope with their problems and indicate why those attempts were not successful. Primary emphasis, however, is on the significance of the Family Group program itself, the particular elements that have been most helpful, and what the program has meant to the individual. Opinions and ideas expressed at a Family Group meeting are solely those of the speakers, not of the fellowship as a whole.

You may be indifferent to some speakers and feel that they have contributed little toward an understanding or solution of *your* problem. Maybe you will disagree strongly with an occasional speaker. These are natural reactions in a fellowship such as ours. But the important thing to remember is that the Family Groups have helped several thousand men and women to achieve a new way of life.[52] If you continue to keep an open mind, you can be helped, too.

Most groups have minor expenses that are defrayed by simply passing the hat. Financial support is wholly voluntary and is not a requirement of membership. The small amounts collected are used to pay for food, literature, rental of a meeting place (in many cases) and to support our over-all service agency, the Al-Anon Family Groups Headquarters.

Organization of local groups is traditionally informal. Usually there is a chairman, a secretary-treasurer and a program committee which arranges meetings. These offices generally rotate among the members. Seldom does a group officer serve for more than six months.[53]

---

52. In 2000 an estimated 387,000 attend Al-Anon meetings.

53. Terms of group offices are up to the autonomy of each group. Service positions beyond the group level are usually for three years.

Each local group is independent, self-directing its own affairs. It is bound to other groups only through the Traditions. Some groups elect to meet weekly, others less frequently. The attendance of most groups consists of non-alcoholics, except for special occasions when alcoholics are invited to attend. Some groups sponsor occasional social affairs.

The growth of Family Groups in the past few years has been astonishing—from 50 groups in 1951 to more than 700 in 1955.[54] However, the early progress of any one group is sometimes painfully slow. This may be discouraging to the original members. Experience suggests, however, that size is not the true measure of the worth of a group. If only two or three members are able to gain help for themselves, or for loved ones, the group must certainly be counted worthwhile. Some groups have continued for months and even years with only a handful of members before attracting large numbers.

No doubt there will always be a few individuals, in isolated areas where no AA or Family Group gatherings are available, who will need to follow the Family Group program by themselves, securing all the help they can through correspondence with the Clearing House and with other Family Groups.

It should also be made clear that, while Family Groups are, of course, associated with Alcoholic Anonymous, they nevertheless remain a distinct entity.

The Twelve Traditions of the Al-Anon Family Groups are approximately the same as those used by the fellowship of Alcoholics Anonymous. They tell how the groups are related to AA, to each other and to the Clearing House. They describe how the movement handles questions of money, property, public relations and anonymity. The Traditions are an over-all guide for unity and function, regarded by most members as indispensable for the survival of our society.

---

54. As of January 1st, 2000 there are 29,800 groups registered worldwide.

THEY FOUND ANSWERS[55]

Let us consider several personal stories which may prove more convincing than anything said so far. Some of the personal commentaries that follow are digests of informal discussions heard at meetings in which older members explain to a newcomer what the program meant to them. One or two have been taken from "The AA Grapevine,"[56] while others are reprints from Family Group literature, issued locally in various sections of the country.[57]

You will find in this section the stories of wives both before and after the alcoholic has found AA. A husband, a parent and two children also tell their experiences:

---

55. See Appendix II, #14 for the 1960 revision to the introduction.

56. *The Grapevine* is Alcoholics Anonymous' monthly magazine

57. Prior to the formation of Al-Anon's World Service Conference, Family Groups published their own literature. Since the early 1960s, all Al-Anon literature has been developed through a Conference Approval process.

Adventure in Growth[58]

Bill started drinking a short time before we were married,[59] and, being alcoholic from the beginning, he got drunk every time he drank. I was greatly concerned by this but felt that our life together would be so complete and full that he would not need an artificial stimulus. But his drinking grew worse as time went on and, since we had no children, my one purpose in life was to help him get over this terrible habit. Aside from his drinking, we were very happy together. We liked the same things and were most companionable.

Finally when the drinking became practically constant, he too, realized he must do something about it and together we tried everything we could think of. He set up all kinds of plans for control; he read psychological books; he went to sanitariums. Twice I gave up my job and we escaped for three months to the country for renewal and rebuilding. Nothing worked. I had had to assume all family responsibilities and make all decisions. It was tragic indeed to see such a fine man so completely beaten and hopeless.

By now we lived entirely to ourselves. We had dropped all our friends or had been dropped by them, and saw as little of our families as possible. Our whole life had simmered down to one terrific fight against alcohol.

Then an old friend whom we had considered a hopeless drunkard came to see Bill to tell of his "release" from alcoholism. Soon the miracle happened and Bill, too, became a changed man, almost overnight. We were happy and grateful—awestruck by this amazing release. Neither of us doubted that it was complete and final. Bill worked endlessly and tirelessly trying to "sober up all the drunks in the world." At least half of these, it seemed to me, in all stages of sobriety, filled our house continually. Since there was as yet no AA,

---

58. Written by Lois W., co-founder of Al-Anon and wife of Bill W., co-founder of AA. This story was revised by Lois in later years and retitled "An Adventure in Growth."

59. Lois dated this as 1918 in the 1960 revision.

we constantly attended meetings of the spiritual group to which our helpful friend belonged.

After a while I began to realize that I was not as happy as I ought to be, that I resented the fact Bill and I had no life together any more, and that I was left alone while he was off somewhere scouting up new drunks or working on old ones. My life's job of sobering up Bill, with all its responsibilities which made me feel so needed, had suddenly vanished and I had not yet found anything to fill the void. Then there was also the feeling of being on the outside of a very tight little clique of alcoholics, where no mere wife could enter. I did not fully understand what was going on within myself until one Sunday Bill asked me if I was ready to go to a meeting with him. To my own surprise as well as his, I burst forth with "Darn your old meeting!"[60] and threw a shoe as hard as I could.

This surprising display of temper woke me up to the fact that I had been wallowing in self-pity. I now could see that Bill's feverish activity with alcoholics was absolutely necessary to his sobriety, and that he had developed spiritually. If I did not want to be left behind, I saw I had better join the procession and strive for much more spiritual growth myself.

Several years later, Bill and I became concerned to find that strained relations, such as ours had been, often developed in families after the first starry-eyed period of AA was over. We were heartsick and puzzled to realize that though many alcoholics were recovering through this wonderful new way of life, their home lives were not always serene. We did not then realize how many adjustments there were to be made, and how much the partner of the alcoholic needed the program, also.

AA now recognizes that alcoholism is a family problem and that recovery can be greatly hastened by family understanding. Groups composed of the families of AAs have sprung up all over the country with a three-fold purpose. First, to give cooperation and under-

---

60. In a later revision Lois wrote, "Damn your old meetings."

standing to the AA member at home. Second, to welcome and give comfort to the families of new or prospective AA members. Third, to live by the Twelve Steps in order to grow spiritually.

AA often speaks of the Twelve Steps as tools. An extension of this idea came to me the other day. There is a striking analogy between working on ourselves in AA or in a Family Group and cultivating a garden.

Our inheritance and early environment compose the soil out of which grow our thoughts and actions, both flowers and weeds. To raise flowers we must get rid of the weeds.

Our garden tools are the knowledge of ourselves and our motives, our honesty in facing ourselves, our desire to help others and our awareness of God. These principles of AA are the tools which we use.

We must keep cultivating with these really effective implements lest our garden be over-run by tares.

Soils vary; some are rocky, sandy, or swampy; others are more fertile. But whatever the soil, there are appropriate flowers that can be grown. Even the desert blooms.

One gardener may find it very difficult to uproot the weeds because his tools are constantly being dulled against the many large rocks in his plot.

But by repeated sharpening of his hoe and by careful selection of his plants he may at last be able to grow a very charming rock garden.

Yet, one who is too sure of the fertility of his plot and takes it for granted that a beautiful garden will be produced because the soil is rich, and therefore doesn't bother to cultivate well, may someday wake up to find the garden filled with insidious weeds that thrive in fertile ground, the weeds of smugness and self-righteousness.

In just this way the garden of many a martyred, self-pitying wife or husband can become choked and therefore unproductive.

The Al-Anon Family Groups show us the need to cultivate the gardens of our lives and how this can be done through the use of AA's Twelve Steps.

The following is how I try to apply these principles to myself:

Step One. We admitted we were powerless over alcohol—that our lives had become unmanageable.

I was just as powerless over my husband's alcoholism as he was, since I failed in every attempt to control his drinking. My own life was indeed unmanageable, as I was forced into doing and being that which I did not want to do or be. I tried to manage Bill's life, although not even able to manage my own. I wanted to get inside his brain and turn the screws in what I thought was the right direction. It took me a long time to see that I, too, was powerless over alcohol.

Step Two. Came to believe that a Power greater than ourselves could restore us to sanity.

Because my thinking was distorted and my nerves overwrought, I held fears and attitudes that certainly were not same. Finally I realized that I, too, had to be restored to sanity and that only by having faith in God, in AA, in my husband and myself, could this come about.

Step Three. Made a decision to turn our will and our lives over to the care of God as we understood him.

Self-sufficiency caused by the habit of acting as mother, nurse, caretaker, and breadwinner, as well as always being considered on the credit side of the ledger with my alcoholic husband on the debit side, resulted in a smug feeling of rightness. At the same time, illogically, I felt a failure at my life's job of helping Bill to sobriety. All this made me blind for a long time to the fact that I needed to turn my will and life over to the care of God. Smugness is the very worst sin of all, I believe. No shaft of light can pierce the armor of self-righteousness.

Step Four. *Made a searching and fearless moral inventory of ourselves.*

Here is where, when I tried to be really honest, I received a tremendous shock. Many of the things that I thought I did unselfishly were, when I tracked them down, pure rationalizations—rationalizations to get my own way about something. This disclosure doubled my urge to live by the Twelve Steps as completely as I could.

Step Five. *Admitted to God, to ourselves, and to another human being the exact nature of our wrongs.*

I found this was just as necessary for me to do as it was for an alcoholic, even more so perhaps, because of my former "mother-and-bad-boy" attitude toward Bill. Admitting my wrongs helped so much to balance our relationship, to bring it closer to the ideal of partnership in marriage.

In the early days I was deeply hurt because someone else had done in a few minutes what I had tried my whole married life to do. Now I have learned that a wife can rarely, if ever, do this job. The sick alcoholic feels his wife's account has been written on the credit side of life's ledger; but he believes his own has been on the debit side. Therefore she cannot possibly understand. Another alcoholic, with a similar debit entry, immediately identifies himself as no non-alcoholic can.

I found no peace of mind until I recognized this important fact.

Step Six. *Were entirely ready to have God remove all these defects of character.*

There were selfish attitudes that I had felt justified in keeping because of what Bill or someone else had done to me. I had to try very hard to want God to remove these. Even after the shoe-throwing episode, my self-pity persisted at losing Bill's companionship and always having the house full of drunks.

Step Seven. *Humbly asked Him to remove our shortcomings.*

"Humbly" was a word I never fully understood. It used to seem servile to me. Today it means seeing myself in true proportion in relation to my fellow man and to God.

While striving for humility myself, it was inspiring to see my husband's growth in the same direction. From an inferiority-ridden person during his drinking days, after AA Bill at first bounced way up to superiority, but he leveled off little by little and gained a very real humility.

Later I saw that it is most natural for alcoholics to rebound from inferiority to superiority when they first join AA. From feeling low, lost, and alone they suddenly find they belong to the most wonderful group of people in the whole world, people who understand, and who are striving to live by the highest principles. Of course, as the newcomer works on the AA program this superiority phase disappears and he begins to grow in humility.

Since I, too, was trying to live the AA program, I had to watch out for my own humility. Slowly and with difficulty I realized I, too, had been beset by both inferiority and superiority. Superiority over Bill in the old days while he was drinking and then inferior to him as he made rapid progress in AA.

Step Eight. *Made a list of all persons we had harmed, and became willing to make amends to them all.*

At first I couldn't think of anyone I had harmed. But when I broke through my own smugness even a little, I saw many relatives and friends whom I had resented and to whom I had given short, irritated answers, imperiling long-standing friendships. In fact, I remember one friend at whom I threw a book when, after a nerve-racking day, he annoyed me. (Throwing seems to have been my pet temper outlet.)

I tried to keep my list of persons harmed up to date, and I also tried to shorten it.

Step Nine. *Made direct amends to such people wherever possible, except when to do so would injure them or others.*

This is just as important for me as for the alcoholic. I found that when I cleaned away the debris of the past by making amends for each harm done, I had taken an important step towards building a bulwark against any hard knocks that later might come along, as well as gaining new serenity and joy in living.

Step Ten. *Continued to take personal inventory and when we were wrong promptly admitted it.*

It is astounding how each time I take an inventory I find some new rationalization, some new way I have been pulling the wool over my own eyes. It is so easy to fool oneself about motives, and admitting it is so hard, but so beneficial.

Step Eleven. *Sought through prayer and meditation to improve our conscious contact with God as we understood Him, praying only for knowledge of His will for us and the power to carry that out.*

I am just beginning to understand how to pray. Bargaining with God is not real prayer and asking him for what I want, even good things, I've had to learn, is not the highest form of prayer. I used to think I knew what was good for me; therefore I, the captain, would give my instructions to my Lieutenant, God, to carry out. That is very different from praying only for the knowledge of God's will and the power for me to carry it out.

Today's living is so involved that much time for meditation is hard to find. But I've set aside a little while night and morning. I am so filled with thankfulness to God that gratitude is one of my principal subjects for meditation; gratitude for all the love and beauty and friends around me, gratitude even for the hard days of long ago that taught me so much. Thus, I have made a start toward improving my conscious contact with God.

Step Twelve. *Having had a spiritual awakening as the result of these steps, we tried to carry this message to others, and to practice these principles in all our affairs.*

I am like many AAs whose spiritual awakening was a slow, developing experience. But I, like all of us, whether our awakening be sudden or gradual, need to continue my efforts toward growth. One either moves forward or slips backward. I sincerely hope there has been a change for the better between my old and new self, and that tomorrow, next month, next year there will continue to be a better new self.

Nothing has done more to urge me forward than the need to carry the AA message to the families of alcoholics who are seeking a way out of their dilemma. The helping of others over the same thorny path that one has already trod strengthens both travelers, the helper and the one being helped.

I "Fed" AA to My Husband[61]

My husband and I turned to AA with a marriage virtually shat-tered by drink. It was held together by the frailest threads—a little hope, a large fear, and two children. The nature of alcoholism was little understood in those days; we certainly did not understand it. Instead, we had fought it, without success. When we sought help in AA we felt we were taking a step in the dark, but we had nowhere else to turn.

In the beginning we sought just one thing, sobriety for my hus-band. We felt that if he were sober, everything else would be adjust-ed and we would be completely happy. My husband soon learned that sobriety in itself was not enough; to achieve a contented sobri-ety, a whole new approach to life was necessary. It didn't take me too long to learn that I, too, had to change my thinking.

At first I made one particular mistake that I hope others can avoid. In my enthusiasm for AA I gulped the program down whole-sale and wanted to feed it back to my husband in small doses. I for-got the "Easy Does It" part of the program, forgot that the initiative had to come from him, not me. My idea of "co-operation" was to rush him past bars and into meetings, all the time telling him what to do to stay sober.

It was not surprising that he had a "slip." I may not have caused his relapse but I certainly was doing nothing to prevent it. It was then that one of the AA wives, a member of the Family Group, sug-gested: "Remember, we all need confidence and faith, confidence in our husbands, and faith in the program itself." I was vulnerable on both points. I really had not had any faith in my husband for years. As for faith in the program, that was a somewhat dubious quality too. But if faith was what I needed, I decided I would conscien-tiously try to develop it. I joined a Family Group and in trying to help others found faith myself.

---

61. This story was removed with the 1960 edition.

A Feminine Joe Louis[62]

Jack was seventeen and I was sixteen when we met. We dated regularly for a year (except when he went on his sprees) and married after he had been sober for three months and had made a sincere promise that he would never drink another drop. I was sure he had quit. After honeymooning 12 days in a nearby city, Jack met an old drinking friend and broke his promise.

Our very first domestic mistake was to move in with his parents, at their insistence. I resented the fact that we did not have our own home, although it was not made an issue. Jack's parents did everything for him financially, but completely dominated his life.

It seemed that he would stand for anything for a while. Then he would fire back with a walloping spree, and he never sobered up until all of us practically fell on our knees to him. Of course, to me, that was a dirty deal.

We were young and very much in love and it was very hard for me to understand why these things happened. I believed him to be sincere and truthful. When I asked him why he did these things I always got the same answer: "I don't know."

He would be gone for days and I would mope in my room feeling sorry for myself and shedding oceans of tears. All I got out of that was red eyes and headaches.

When our first son was born, I was sure Jack would have enough love and respect for us to stop drinking. But he was so drunk by the time our son came into the world he didn't know a baby from a monkey. He stayed drunk more than he ever had before. You see, then, I could think it was nothing but cussedness on his part.

When we discovered there was to be a second child we moved into our own home. I was sure Jack would stay sober. He would be so completely happy. It was our first home after almost seven years of marriage. We were very happy for a few weeks. Then he threw a

62. This story was removed with the 1960 edition.

drunk that capped all up to that time. I quit crying and started fighting. During this period of about a year, we really had some scenes. I got the name of Joe Louis.

Every time I thought we were going fine he would upset things with another spree. This went on for seven or eight years, with Jack being drunk always when he was needed. Every child we had was greeted in this world by a drunken father either at the time or short-ly after. I gave up hope and became a martyr. We never talked much. We were almost strangers. Of course, he was sure I had stopped loving him, and I had the same opinion concerning him.

Then he was drafted. After two years in the service, he decided he had reformed. He made all sorts of promises to God and me—after several narrow escapes in battle. He did reform for about seven months. Then he got upset and threw a drunk that really set us back and sent me to the hospital. You see, I had gained hope again, only to lose it in one thundering episode. This time there were no fights, no fusses between us. I just died all over in a few hours. I didn't have time to adjust myself gradually as I had done before.

While in the hospital, I made a resolution that I would return to my church work. I had been an active church worker before mar-riage and immediately after. I read my Bible daily and found com-fort I had long wanted.

I decided I had done the best I could do. I would leave the rest to God. I promised myself that I would never be sick again over such things as had put me in the hospital, because my children needed me too badly. We had four at that time.

After that, when Jack got drunk, he was strictly on his own. I just saw to it that the children were subjected to as little trouble as pos-sible.

Jack heard of AA in February 1949. One more short spree, then he went on the program.

Now we live an entirely different life. Jack joined the church after a few months, and is now one of its leaders. We have found happiness in turning our will over to God, happiness that I never thought possible.

We both attend AA meetings, never missing except for illness. In the Family Group I found that it was as important for me to live the Twelve Steps as for him.

I just can't put into words what our new life means to our family. It is just as if we had been in a dark tunnel all these years and had just emerged to the beauty of the rising sun.

We will always be grateful to AA and the Family Group—only God knows how grateful. We accept the fact that Jack will always be an alcoholic and that, but for the grace of God, our lives and the lives of our children would have been ruined.

Alcohol Is Not My Problem[63]

I have made a startling discovery: alcohol is not my problem. Alcohol can only be the problem of an alcoholic. However, through living with an alcoholic over a period of years, I became as sick mentally, physically and spiritually as he.

My husband's illness has a definite name and treatment—*he* is an alcoholic and Alcoholics Anonymous is his program of recovery. My maladjustment was a little more difficult to name and treat, but I was definitely neurotic.

I do not know all the answers to the problems that wives, husbands and parents are called on to solve, except through my own personal experience and through the association of those who have had the same problems.

---

63. The original story is presented here. Minor revisions were made by the original writer in the March 1966 edition.

Today I am grateful for all the experiences I have had. I am deeply grateful for the privilege of associating with others in the Family Group who have had similar experiences because I have learned that the love and friendship which is the basis of our lives, and our way of life, needs the *best* we have, *all* the time.

I do know that for every alcoholic, there is a wife or husband, often children and a mother and father, whose lives have become as involved as that of the alcoholic himself. If I can help one man or woman to deal realistically with his or her alcoholic mate, then I may have helped that alcoholic, and at the same time given hope and encouragement to his loved ones.

Knowing nothing about Alcoholics Anonymous and much less about alcoholism, my mental processes deteriorated as rapidly as those of my husband. Gradually losing all the fine things we had hoped and planned for, and had within our grasp, developed in me a confusion which continued to engulf me with each succeeding failure in my attempts to help him.

Throughout all these bad times, there did remain within me a faith, a faith that sometime, somehow, something would help my husband find himself and be the fine person I knew and loved in his sober time. There is a dominant force in our lives that refuses to let us abandon our mates, even in the darkest hours.

With the advent of AA in our lives, that faith gave rise to hope and when we dared hope, our confusion and despair began to vanish. We could begin to think with clear minds.

Ill in mind and body, I found myself in a hospital, recovering from major surgery. Despite well-meant promises not to drink at that time, my husband drank himself into one of the other hospitals on a ten-day bender. This was the physical and mental low for us. While in the hospital I was informed that my husband had been contacted by Alcoholics Anonymous at his own request, and that he believed he had found a way out. My immediate reaction was one of a "tongue-in-cheek" disbelief. By this time I cared little what happened.

Coincident with my convalescence, my husband soberly and eagerly attended AA meetings. For the first time I heard him say, "I can never drink again. I am an alcoholic." Believe me, I was still a long way from being convinced that anyone or anything could ever help him. I had had a thousand promises in a thousand different ways. I was afraid to believe. I don't think I shall ever forget the day, shortly after I came home from the hospital, when two Family Group members, wives of AAs, came to see me, two happy women who said, "Six months from now you'll be laughing at this." Fortunately, I had neither the strength nor the brickbats to wield that day.

With my recovery and first attendance at an AA meeting, I began casting about for information about alcoholism. At Family Group meetings I learned through listening to the experiences of other non-alcoholic mates that, by utilizing the Fourth of the Twelve Steps, I could discover many distinct neurotic tendencies in myself, acquired in my days and years of dark confusion.

The Fourth Step, which reads, "Made a searching and fearless moral inventory of ourselves," is a real challenge to honesty with one's self. We all find it so easy and pleasant to view ourselves through a rosy hue of complimentary half-truths, and so hard and unpleasant to take a look in the uncompromising and glaring light of the unvarnished truth. If I were to help my husband in his efforts to recover, I could do so only in effecting my own mental recovery. I saw my husband daily striving to live a program of deep spiritual regeneration and I knew I must do likewise.

Here came the fruition of that deep faith that has sustained me! My sincere desire to help would no longer be doomed to disappointment. I needed only to improve myself. From that day to this the principles and philosophy of the AA program have been the governing influence in our lives. I removed my tongue from my cheek and put my nose in the AA book and Family Group literature. I was convinced that something wonderful was happening in my life. It was then I saw, I heard, I believed. Thus came hope.

We must realize that the recovery of our own mental health and attitudes does not occur overnight, no more so than the recovery of our alcoholic mates. Even as they, we can only grow by learning and applying to our own lives the principles of the AA way of life. How many times in our despair we have said, "I would do anything if my husband would only stop drinking"? Now is our opportunity to prove our sincerity by continuous action to do the only thing in which we can reasonably hope to succeed: improve ourselves, our home lives and our spiritual attitudes.

We gradually understand we must relinquish the martyr role for one of a more realistic nature in the light of our philosophy of living. Many adjustments must be made in our transition from a person wronged to that of a person who may have *been* wrong. It is our obligation to learn the difference and there is only one way to do that: "Know thyself!"

Honest, sincere study and application of the AA and Family Group program, coupled with the friendship and fellowship of those who have shared our experiences, provides a regeneration of body, mind and spirit. It is the spirit of the AA philosophy that catches and holds the interest of the alcoholic and non-alcoholic alike.

It is because of this spirit, this influence, that the alcoholic grasps that life-line in his search for release from physical pain and the attainment of peace of mind and serenity of heart and soul. The non-alcoholic has shared in this search. I believe that a person who attains peace of mind is well on the way to recovery from any maladjustment. He who possesses peace of mind must assuredly possess an honest faith in a Power greater than himself, faith in himself and in those about him.

"To thine own self be true, and it must follow as the night the day thou canst not then be false to any man."[64] This is not just a trite saying. We must be absolutely courageous in our honesty to ourselves. We are attempting to keep stride with an individual who must practice rigid honesty in all things. Deceit has no place in his life and is therefore more easily recognized in the actions of others.

There is a humorous story of a conversation between a pastor and a member of AA. The pastor inquired, "Don't you have hypocrites in AA"? To which the AA member replied, "Yes, but we have it on you. We can *smell* ours."

Constant or recurring self-pity for wrongs or fancied wrongs that may have happened in the past is negative. You might just as well close the door on yesterday because it is gone. It is too late to go through that day again. We are happiest when, in spite of discouragement, we put up a good home front. It is an exacting task, not made up of occasional glamorous gestures, but of a steady self-discipline, sensitive awareness of what hurts, what irritates, what displeases.

When our self-pity takes the form of criticizing the former character defects of our alcoholic mates (before AA) which he is now striving to overcome, it might be well to take the recommendation of the Sioux Indians, "Oh, Great Spirit, help me never to judge another until I have walked two weeks in his moccasins." A friend of mine also showed me that each time I used a finger to point out a fault in someone else, three fingers point back at me.

Each of us will come a long way when we can approach every activity in our lives with the AA prayer[65] ever in mind: "God, grant me (not only my husband) the serenity to accept the things I cannot change, courage to change the things I can (mostly me) and wisdom to know the difference." Just for twenty-four hours!

---

64. This quote is from Shakespeare's *Hamlet*.
65. The Serenity Prayer was formerly referred to as The AA Prayer.

Team Work[66]

I came to the Family Group as beaten mentally and spiritually as my husband, the alcoholic, came to AA. For every year he had of drinking, I had a year of trying to combat all the frustrations and resentments that go with living with an alcoholic. While he had hangovers from drinking, I had hangovers from thinking. While he tried running away from his responsibilities, I was running, too, but in every direction.

When he took his illness out on me, I took mine out on the children. I loved him. I hated him. I wished he would have an accident and I was terrified that he would. When he spent money, I saved like a martyr; and when he, during a sober period, tried to save to make up, I blew the works. When he was drunk, I wanted him sober. Yet many times I told him to go out and get drunk. When he was pleasant, I was not.

We were not a team in any sense of the word.

My need for the principles of AA was as great as his.

Gradually as our daily living of this joint program began to straighten out the little problems, I came to realize that I had all my defects of character before I had the alcoholic. I stopped running and slowed to a walk, greeting each day with renewed hope and faith. I began to learn about self-discipline, to be aware of the needs of others, to listen more and talk less, to keep an open mind, and have more tolerance.

There certainly has been a very great change in my attitude toward the problem, my husband and my family.

Through this way of life, we have become a team again. I now have a personal awareness of the Twelve Steps and know that I must work each and every Step by myself and for myself alone. I cannot be part of a working team if I do not carry my share of the load and let the other half carry his.

---

66. This story was removed with the 1960 edition.

A new understanding of God has come to me even though these years of sobriety and of living the principles of AA in the home have not been without their problems. Three and a half years ago I was faced with the grave illness of my husband, which still necessitates constant nursing. His sudden blindness two years later took considerable adjustment on my part but I have been able to meet it with loving kindness. The loss of a son in Korea was a profound lesson in acceptance which, with God's help, I am still trying to learn. My care of our other son and our home is done now with considerably more tolerance and understanding.

Through this philosophy, I am able to live a daily life of happiness and gratitude. I am learning to live in the present and to be happy with those with whom I live and work. I am grateful for this new way of life and the privilege of helping others, with a completely new understanding of my own and their problems.

I feel that I have become a wife and mother again, and am part of the team.

Fear No Evil[67]

Al's drinking career was active for fifteen to twenty years. His association with AA was from 1943-1950 before "it" took. He has been sober not quite five years—the most wonderful of years.

I had so much to learn, for during Al's drinking I had unconsciously given him the power to do evil and, equally unconsciously, had taken unto myself the power to correct this condition, or attempt to.

In Psalms 62:11 it says, "God hath spoken once, twice have I heard this: that power belongeth unto God." And so I had to take

---

67. This story was removed with the 1960 edition.

that first Step and acknowledge and accept my powerlessness over Al and alcohol. I had to place the power, for good, where it belonged, with God. Then I reasoned that if there was a Higher Power who would and could help an alcoholic only when this Step is sincerely taken, this same Power must be ready to help me, regardless of whether I had, intentionally or unintentionally, done wrong.

One evening I heard an AA speaker say he had had trouble believing in a Power that was interested in him and he was told to *pretend* there was. He did, and the results were so wonderful, he had to believe. So that's what I did.

Living with an active alcoholic doesn't give you a very cherished feeling, so whenever anything troubled me regarding members of my family or conditions, I would talk it over silently with that wonderful Power, tell Him what was troubling me and thank Him for taking care of me. I have slowly learned that if God can tell me what is right to do, He can tell my family and He doesn't need me as an interpreter.

I apply everything I can learn in AA and in the Family Group, to my daily life. You hear, "this might be called a selfish program, for you have to want it yourself before you can pass it on." So each morning I pray for guidance for myself and each evening I say, "Thank you." Actually I do this many times a day. And just as the alcoholic's "selfish" prayers benefit him and hence everyone he comes in contact with, so my prayers are being answered by a family life that is just plain wonderful.

To me the whole philosophy of the Twelve Steps is tied up in two Psalms. The first is: "Be still, and know that I am God." Here he gives us two directives and both have to be followed for best results. And the second Psalm is: "I will fear no evil, for Thou art with me."

It's a wonderful, wonderful program!

His Way, Not Mine[68]

I have lived now for twenty-three years with an alcoholic. Had I known anything at all about alcoholism that long time ago, things might have been different. My mother was concerned about Jim's drinking when we were engaged, but I assured her she needn't worry—he could stop any time. I was sure he could because he said so.

When it continued, and worsened, after we were married, I went through all the phases: blaming myself for it, trying to prevent it, trying to hide it and making myself generally into a person totally unlike my former self.

Finally, about eight years ago, I was desperately unhappy and no longer willing to live such a dreary life. From somewhere I remembered hearing about AA and spoke that familiar piece about "It's AA, or else." So, for a time, it was AA. For almost a year, after initial difficulty, AA *was* the answer and we attended meetings regularly. For the first time I found a place where I could speak freely to other wives.

The things I heard in meetings were totally new to me. If I had read things in newspapers about jails, crimes or misbehavior, I had never related them to drinking. I had had no notion that over-indulgence in alcohol was an illness. It was a comfort to learn that Jim was not entirely responsible for his conduct.

But before the year was over, so was my new-found peace. And all that I had heard in other men's stories came back to haunt me ten-fold. A wet-brain was something new to worry about; so was the worry of Jim's assaulting someone when he was not responsible and didn't even know what he was doing; the idea of preventing the first drink became my first thought. I was the complete eager beaver in selling the program to him.

---

68. This story was retitled "But for the Grace of Al-Anon" in 1966 and revised in later editions as noted in Appendix II, #15.

I certainly know that life with an alcoholic is most difficult for those who have children. I tried my best to protect my child from the effects of her father's excessive drinking. For I did want my child to have a normal home, a decent place for friends to visit, and a father she could respect.

For the next five years I moved heaven and earth to help my husband find sobriety. It is needless to say here that nothing that I did helped and most of it harmed. When I heard the Al-Anon Family Group's Clearing House needed volunteers, I went, not to help myself, but because I had been told the two or three working there were struggling to do a job which would swamp a dozen. For the first time, some real appreciation of my situation began to dawn on me.

Because the AA program had been presented to me as a way of life for alcoholics, I had not thought to live it myself. I had merely recognized it as a wonderful philosophy for alcoholics, a blueprint for a way to sobriety. But at the Clearing House I learned that Family Groups all over the world were living it themselves, non-alcoholics getting mentally sober through the Steps. I joined a Family Group and learned more of the program as it applied to me.

But for me the First Step was the most difficult. I admitted I was powerless over alcohol but I did not accept all its implications. In my mind was always the nagging thought that there was something I hadn't yet tried that would work magic for us. And so I went on, living the program in part. And consequently I gained only part of the benefit.

After several years in the Family Groups, I really took that First Step. I cannot say what enabled me to do so—perhaps it just took that long for me to learn exactly how powerless I am. Perhaps I had to suffer the extra time in order to really appreciate what havoc I was adding to an already difficult situation. But with taking of that Step, the rest fell into place. I've often watched our cat and thought how much like him I was. He continually catches sight of his tail, bites it and then lets go quickly when it hurts. The only difference between me and the cat is that I held on so long, hurting myself so constantly.

When I took the First Step, I, for the first time, really looked to God for help. Before that I had been occupied with telling Him what to do, how to do it, and please to do it quickly. I'd always said "Thy Will be done" but hadn't thought I was still striving for my own will. My will, since I was asking only for peace, decency and a normal home, seemed all right to live by.

Now I am willing to believe I didn't earn congratulations for the way I had lived my life, and that God could do a better job of running it. I saw that if I hadn't fought against alcoholism, that problem might have been solved earlier. I had made Jim obstinate by pushing too hard. If I had just given up earlier in my efforts to control his drinking, our home would have been more tranquil, at least by the measure of my own acceptance and serenity.

We are still living with the problem. Perhaps Jim is one of the unfortunate few who will never get the program. That is not for me to say, just as I cannot say how long I can continue life under present conditions. But I am now able to live with more grace, more acceptance and more happiness. The times between bouts are not clouded with worry about the next episode. I have learned to live through his binges by detaching myself from them. I have learned not to scold, make scenes, become depressed, nor to chase after Jim. I have stopped pouring out liquor, have stopped sleeping on the floor in front of the door so he can't get out for more. I have stopped all the useless schemes I used to try.

I have learned to trust that God in His own time will help us both, as He sees fit, and that no matter what happens, it is possible to be a better person for having lived through these difficult years. There are a lot of things I'd be glad to have changed in my life—I'd like to be free of debt; I'd like to have a little more financial security and I'd like to have a husband who is always himself. But I have learned that just living is not the most important thing. I am concentrating on *how* to live my life as it is, and not necessarily as I'd like to live it.

With the help of God and the Family Group Steps, I am constantly trying to live His way—and not mine.

The Beginning Of Understanding

I am the wife of an alcoholic. When I first came to the Family Group I was defeated, fearful, lonely and frustrated. Resentment filled my thinking; it warped my judgment and paralyzed my usefulness. Because my own problem filled my mind so completely, I found myself forgetting appointments, going blocks past my bus stop, looking at people and not hearing what they said.

When no one in the group said anything about how to deal with my alcoholic husband, I was surprised and disappointed. I was shocked and even more resentful at the suggestion that perhaps I might need some reconditioning of my own thinking and way of living.

That phase passed. As I learned more, I began to appreciate that I actually was powerless over alcohol, even as my husband seemed to be, and that it made sense to turn this problem over to a Power greater than myself. That was the beginning of my understanding of the importance of the first two suggested Steps in the AA program which apply so perfectly to non-alcoholics like ourselves. This understanding brought peace of mind and a new joy in living I would not have believed possible. Yet nothing had changed but my own attitude.

I used to wonder why *my* prayers were never answered. Now I can see that they were completely selfish, that I was not ready, spiritually, for them to be answered. How could I expect to have answers to my prayers when I was filled with enmity[69], self-pity and resentment?

I became aware of my own defects and what I could do to change them. I Let Go and Let God. I substituted positive thoughts for negative ones—love for enmity, praise for criticism, forgiveness in place of resentment. Working the Family Group program on a twenty-four hour basis, with daily time for prayer and meditation, gave me new confidence and faith. And I have found, as I was told I would, that "right answers" do come when you put your mind on "being" rather than on "getting."

Helpful Reality

When I say that I am the most grateful woman alive and that the alcoholic problem is still unsolved in our home, you may think I don't know what gratitude means. But I am truly grateful for what a "Power greater than myself," working through the Family Group, has done for me.

I once lived in a state of despair and defeat. My fear for my husband—for what alcohol was doing to him—amounted to panic. Not understanding that his drinking was a symptom of illness, I was filled with resentment and self-pity. I was literally a sick person myself.

Then I heard of AA but could not interest my husband in it. One day I asked an AA member if the program had helped him. His brief answer startled me. "God has helped me," he said. I was unprepared for such an answer. Previously, when someone had brought God

---

69. Enmity was changed to "hostility" in 1966.

into a conversation, I had been uneasy and embarrassed. But when this man spoke of God as a helpful reality, it did more for me than all the sermons I had ever heard.

I began to believe that if God could help this man, He could help me. As soon as possible I sought out the Family Group. I shall always be grateful for the heart-warming friendliness of those women who had been through the same experience I had. There was no need to elaborate my troubles to them, or to try to hide them. Everyone understood. It meant that I could relax and be natural. The small spark of courage and hope kindled by my first AA friend was fanned into flame.

My greatest help came when my new friends told me: "Take your hands off your husband's life entirely. Turn that problem over to God, as you understand Him. Then begin to do something about your own life."

I was told that my life would change in proportion to the honest effort I made to change it. I said to myself: "If that is the secret of the serenity I see in the faces of these people, that is what I want." I had reached the end of my rope; I was absolutely defeated and discouraged. I was ready to do anything those kind people suggested.

I found that trying *not* to run my husband's life was easier said than done. Dreading disaster, fearful for his safety, I had been trying for years to save him from himself. Today I realize that this attitude had probably only made things worse. And when I wanted with all my heart to Let Go and Let God, I found myself bound by years of wrong habits.

The change in me and in my attitude came very gradually. I often had to learn to control my tongue when angry. I had to learn not to question erratic comings and goings. I had to ignore evidence of drinking. I had to put aside doubts that everything would turn out for the best. Over and over, I had to remind myself, "He is in the hands of a Power greater than I am; things will work out."

Gradually I discovered that concern over the alcoholic problem no longer occupied my mind to the complete exclusion of other things. I began to experience a feeling of release. I know that I was free of a burden and responsibility that were too heavy for me. I sensed that our lives were being guided by a Power that was infinite and loving. I felt a lightening and buoyancy of spirit that brought with it a strong sense of security. Finally I realized, "Why, I really am as free as the air." It was a tremendous feeling.

Formerly, every reminder of my husband's drinking set off a terrific surge of bitterness and resentment. I learned that I had to overcome this weakness. I did, but I can't claim all the credit. Today, when I ask for help from the Higher Power we speak of in the Family Group, I can feel a change within myself. The hateful emotions are replaced by patience and loving kindness. I find it easier to live with myself since I have replaced negative thoughts with positive ones. It should not be difficult to understand the gratitude I feel. For I am grateful for the opportunity to learn and live this new way of life.

Practicing These Principles[70]

My wife and I had a few happy years together when an accident, resulting in a miscarriage, changed everything and she became an alcoholic. Our lives changed abruptly, but at first I didn't appreciate what had happened. I simply knew that our house was always a mess, that I could never be sure that Mary would be sober when I got home and that we could never entertain friends or go visiting. I hated all of it.

---

70. This story was removed with the 1960 edition.

Money made the most trouble. Mary could no longer be trusted with it. Every cent she got hold of seemed to go for liquor. Things got so bad I had to do all the shopping for food, household supplies, even her clothes.

One day I ran into an old friend who had once been a complete lush, and found that he had been sober for several years. He told me about AA and when I told Mary about him, she said she was willing to try the program. To help her, I sought out the local Family Group, as a sort of last concession.

What I heard about turning my problem over to a Power greater than myself puzzled me at first. A spiritual approach like that had never made much sense to me in the past. But when I gave it some thought, I saw that I had been trying to do everything all by myself, and that approach certainly hadn't worked. No one had ever elected me to run the world but that was precisely what I had been trying to do for the two of us for years. If marriage is a partnership, I had reached the point where all I wanted was a silent partner.

When I decided to just run my own life, with the help of a Higher Power, I was able to relax for the first time in years. I suddenly appreciated that I was not so perfect that I could set myself up as a model for Mary. I even came to appreciate that she had been really ill and that she needed help that I had never given her.

Today we are working the AA program and the Family Group program together. While I can't say that I never raise my voice any more, I can say that our life isn't the terrible thing it once was. And I know that by "practicing these principles" in all my affairs, my own relations with everyone have improved. I am doing better at my job. I have more friends who like me better. And we both have a home instead of a private hell.

A Father Works It Out[71]

I am the father of an alcoholic, a boy who now no longer drinks, thanks to AA. Anyone who knew me in the days when Bob was drinking will appreciate that mothers and wives aren't the only ones who suffer in a home where a loved one is a problem drinker.

I have dragged my son out of bars and forced him to come home with me. Other times, waiting for him to return, I have paced the floor hours on end, hot with anger and resentment.

A doctor told me Bob had an illness, but I thought he was simply excusing the boy. But the doctor also told me about AA; he thought it could help. After making some inquiries, I began going to open meetings—alone. For a long period, Bob refused to go, but I attended regularly. In those days there were no Family Groups, but I soon came to appreciate that the doctor was right; alcoholism was an illness. I stopped chasing after Bob and taking his money and liquor away. I realized that he would have to want to stop drinking before I could help him. I recognized that the first important thing was to change my own attitude and stop fighting my son.

After a while, Bob began to go to AA meetings with me. He must have sensed the change in my approach. Whatever the reason, AA made sense to him right away. He hasn't had a drink since.

When I first heard of Family Groups, I wanted to be a part of this new fellowship. I knew how much they could have helped me, had they been in existence during the days when Bob was drinking. I thought, too, that I could help others by passing along my experience in working with an alcoholic close to me. And, finally, I realized how much I still had to learn about living with a recovered alcoholic.

The Serenity Prayer has meant a great deal to me. Deciding what I can and cannot change has made a big difference in my life. My doctor tells me that high blood pressure, or heart strain, will never

---

71. In 1960 this story was re-titled "Sobriety and My Son." See Appendix II, #16.

bother me now. I simply do the best I can and leave it at that. If some other person's best is better than mine, mine is still best for me.

Instead of alienating my son, as I had rapidly been doing, we are closer together than ever. His wife and his children are once more truly a part of our family. If it had not been for the change in myself, and the results it helped to produce in my boy, there would have been a wall between us that nothing could ever have torn down.

A Daughter Is Proud Of Her AA Mother[72]

I am proud to say that I am a daughter of a member of Alcoholics Anonymous. Indeed, I am proud to be the daughter of a true alcoholic, for it makes my mother seem like a special kind of person. I cannot say that I have always felt this way. No one could who has grown up with an alcoholic. Certainly AA brings a happier life to the family and a wonderful new beginning for the alcoholic. It brings a realization that it wasn't her fault; she didn't do it just to be mean; she had an illness that somehow made her allergic to alcohol.

I realize that no matter how perfect the picture now is, there are still hurts and resentments inside of me, covered over, repressed. All the many years that I was told, "Mummy isn't quite herself today," when I was afraid to bring friends home from school because "Mummy might be that way again today"—these wounds cannot be wiped out overnight.

And I think this is important for a parent to remember. The alcoholic cannot recall the things she has said and done while drinking. She often cannot understand why her children do not trust and respect her. It takes a long time to gain back the respect of a child. It will be difficult to wipe out the wounds of these childhood experiences, but they can be wiped out.

---

72. This story was removed with the 1960 edition.

It took me more than a year before I could live pleasantly with my family again. There was so much resentment and antagonism that I could not understand what the AA philosophy was or what it meant in my life. It is important for the alcoholic to work slowly toward a new relationship, and not to expect an immediate change in the child's attitude. It is even more important for the child to study the AA program. Through this she will realize that her mother was not to blame, and a much richer fuller relationship can develop than exists in most families. Many of my school friends have mothers who are very neurotic, or very domineering, or who live with families where there is some great conflict. I think I am more fortunate than they are, because many of their problems may never be solved.

The remarkable thing about the problem of alcoholism in the family is that, when the alcoholic becomes sober permanently, your solution is there—concrete, visible.

As I learned of the basic, humane ideas embodied in the AA program, as I saw great changes in my mother, I was able to develop our relationship until today it is a perfection of unity and closeness. I realize now that we were never fighting each other, but struggling together against an unknown enemy. Through this struggle and the comradeship that comes with solving something together, we are happier than we might have been if this problem of alcoholism had never entered our lives.

The friends I used to envy, those with an everyday, normal, wholesome life, take their families for granted. I cannot feel that way because there is something very special and inspiring about our new family relationship. Perhaps it's the kind of feeling parents get when their pilot son has been reported lost at sea, and then a sudden message reports that he has drifted to land and safety. It's the special quality of joy one gets when something very precious has been lost for a long time and suddenly found again.

I Needed The Twelve Steps[73]

It took me one year and a half, besides a shattering experience, to learn that I had only been interested in the program—not living it as I had thought.

Since my father was an alcoholic before I was born, I have lived my whole twenty-one years with the problem in the family, but it didn't affect me much. I can remember that I could always tell by the way Daddy put his key in the door whether he was all right or not. If he weren't, I'd run quickly to my room and shut the door because I didn't want to be around him. I couldn't have liked the situation much.

But I couldn't always avoid him at such times. Mother worried a lot, but when this happened I told her not to get upset. I explained that when he'd been drinking I didn't consider him my father, that I had absolutely no respect for him then, so it didn't matter what he did. The minute he was himself, he was my real father again and everything was fine.

Mother couldn't understand this Jekyll-Hyde business and was afraid that sometime I'd not be able to switch back. When she and Dad discovered AA, she told me all about it as fast as she learned herself. I was eleven then. Dad had prolonged difficulty with the program—skipped in and out as if it had revolving doors.

Then, three years ago, Mommie heard of the Family Group. It did wonders for her because the strain had been awful. During a vacation from college almost two years ago, when Daddy was drinking, she asked if I didn't want to go to a meeting with her. To make her feel good, I went. I loved it. I was most impressed by the attitude of the members and their sincerity. I thought I'd live the program, too. I never missed a meeting after that when I was home from school. I thought I was living the Steps.

73. This story was removed with the 1960 edition.

A year ago Daddy went on an awful binge and I was alone in the house with him one afternoon. I didn't like the way he acted and thought I'd really scare him, perhaps end the whole problem. I packed a bag and went to stay with a friend. While there I ran into a family friend, an AA woman, and I told her what had happened. She said she'd often thought Mommie had cushioned things too much for Daddy so that he'd never "reached bottom," that neither of them had ever really taken the First Step. When I came home, I told Mommie and said I thought it would help if she'd learn the same kind of detachment our AA friend had. After that, every time Mommie worried about Dad having a slip, I'd remind her to be detached. I must have been awful to live with.

But the whole thing boiled up this summer. I had a job in the college shop of a department store and one afternoon I was sick and was sent home. I dragged home, hardly able to make it. When I got there I couldn't get in because I'd forgotten my key for the only time this summer. I rang and rang, and then got the superintendent's wife to let me in the empty apartment next door where I could see into the bedrooms. They were empty so I thought no one was home. I tried half an hour to get out a corridor window onto a ledge so I could climb across to our kitchen window, but the window stuck and I couldn't budge it. Then the superintendent came along, opened it, got a ladder and went in himself to let me in the door.

I was frantic by then, but the whole mess really got to me when I saw Daddy asleep on the davenport. I cried for an hour. Daddy went out some time while I was crying. When he came back, he couldn't get his key in the keyhole so he rang and rang. And I would not let him in.

Then Mommie called up to say she'd be late, and asked how Daddy was. I said I didn't know, he'd been ringing the bell for twenty minutes and could keep on ringing. She said, "Let him in," and I said, "No—I want him to see how it feels." Mommie was horrified: "Let him in. You *know* he's a sick man." So I did.

I was getting some orange juice in the kitchen when she came home. I thought I had myself well in hand until she asked me what had happened. That was too much. I picked up a lid of a pan and threw it as hard as I could across the kitchen, yelling, "He's a brute—he's lost his mind, and I don't want any part of him."

Mommie told me not to yell, that I wasn't practicing the program, that it was because I was sick myself that I was so upset. "Program!" I screamed. "That's a lot of glop. That's for morons. It's all just *words*. They don't know what Daddy's like."

Mommie kept on and said to let it all out of my system to her, but that she *knew* the program worked. If it worked for her, it would work for me.

Suddenly something she said made sense to me and in one flash I realized I had never taken the First Step myself; I had continued to think I could influence him. And I had gotten so furious because things had happened to me personally this time, while before I had only got them in a sort of reflected way because Mommie had shielded me from the worst of them.

I saw that I needed to practice the Steps. I had been *interested* before in an academic way, but now I knew I *needed* them for myself. I began right then with the First [Step] and I've been working on the rest of them. Since then I've gone through two of Dad's binges, and I think that pan lid is the last thing I'll toss in anger.

Perhaps it took an outburst like that to show me how superficially I'd been taking the Family Group before. All I know is that things are different now and when I need help I know where to get it.

APPENDIX[74]

This appendix contains the following useful material:

Part I — Family Group Meetings

Part II — Traditions

Part III — Group Structure

Part IV — Literature

74. This is the Appendix from the original book.

Part I — Family Group Meetings[75]

Suggested Welcome[76]

We welcome you to the Al-Anon Family Group and hope that in this fellowship you will find the help and friendship we have been privileged to enjoy. We would like you to feel that we understand as perhaps few can. We, too, were lonely and frustrated, but here we have found that there is no situation too difficult to be bettered, and no unhappiness too great to be lessened.

Suggested Preamble To The Twelve Steps[77]

The Al-Anon Family Groups consist of relatives and friends of alcoholics who realize that by banding together they can better solve their common problems. Both before and after the alcoholic joins AA, there is much that families can do to help the alcoholics and themselves.

We urge you to try our program. Without spiritual help, living with an alcoholic is too much for most of us. We become nervous, irritable, unreasonable—our thinking becomes confused, and our perspective becomes distorted. A change in our attitude is of boundless help to the AA member and often is the force for good that finally inspires the alcoholic to join AA. So there is no need for discouragement even though the alcoholic is still drinking.

Rarely have we seen a family that was not greatly benefited when both husband and wife tried to live the AA program. Working in unity for a common purpose does more than strengthen both partners individually. It also draws them together.

The Twelve Steps of AA, which we try to follow, are not easy. At first we may think that some of them are unnecessary, but if we are thoroughly honest with ourselves, we will find that they all apply to us as well as to the alcoholic. The benefit derived from a strict and

---

75. Title was changed in March 1960 to "Al-Anon Family Group Fundamentals."

76. See Appendix II, # 17 for revised wording.

77. See Appendix II, #18a and #18b for subsequent text revisions.

constant observance of them can be limitless. We thus make ourselves ready to receive God's gift of serenity.

Here are the steps which are suggested as a program of growth:

Twelve Steps

1. We admitted we were powerless over alcohol—that our lives
   had become unmanageable.

2. Came to believe that a Power greater than ourselves could
   restore us to sanity.

3. Made a decision to turn our will and our lives over to the care
   of God *as we understood Him.*

4. Made a searching and fearless moral inventory of ourselves.

5. Admitted to God, to ourselves, and to another human being
   the exact nature of our wrongs.

6. Were entirely ready to have God remove all these defects of
   character.

7. Humbly asked Him to remove our shortcomings.

8. Made a list of all persons we had harmed, and became willing
   to make amends to them all.

9. Made direct amends to such people wherever possible, except
   when to do so would injure them or others.

10. Continued to take personal inventory and when we were wrong
    promptly admitted it.

11. Sought through prayer and meditation to improve our conscious
    contact with God, *as we understood Him,* praying only for
    knowledge of His will for us and the power to carry that out.

12. Having had a spiritual awakening as the result of these steps,
    we tried to carry this message to others, and to practice these
    principles in all our affairs.

Varieties of Meetings

Most Family Group meetings are conducted like AA meetings. In many groups the leader or chairman opens the meeting with a moment of silence and a welcome, followed by a reading of the Preamble and the Twelve Steps. The meetings take various forms, a number of which are listed below. The meeting is then closed by a unison repetition of the Lord's Prayer.[78]

Suggested types of meetings follow:

1. *Personal Story Meeting*—Two or three speakers have been asked beforehand by the leader to tell how they came to believe the AA program was a way of life for them as well as the alcoholic. (Care, of course, being taken not to blame the alcoholic.)

2. *Twelve Steps Meeting*—The group takes up one of the Twelve Steps at a meeting, members discussing the application of that step to themselves.

3. *Forum Discussions*—Group members are invited to write questions, which are then answered either by a panel of two or three members chosen by the leader or by anyone caring to.

4. *AA Speaker Meeting*—An occasional invitation to an AA member to address the group is interesting, his talk being directed to the necessary adjustments and cooperation at home, rather than his alcoholic story.[79]

5. *Family-Adjustment Meeting*—Husband and wife teams (one an alcoholic, the other a non-alcoholic) discuss the problems of home adjustments after the alcoholic joins AA.

6. *Visiting Groups*—If there are any other Family Groups in your vicinity, invite a team of speakers to address your meetings occasionally.

---

78. See Appendix II, #19 for current suggested closing.

79. See the *Al-Anon/Alateen Service Manual*, "Groups at Work" section, Meeting Ideas.

7. *Outside Speakers*—Physicians, members of the clergy, court workers, etc., can be asked to address a meeting.[80]

8. *Inspirational Literature*—The application of the AA Prayer[81] to
   every day living may be considered. Perhaps the current issue of
   the Family Group periodical, the Family Group Forum,[82] could
   be read and discussed. Any other inspirational literature agreeable to all can be taken up for discussion.[83]

9. *Open Meetings*—It is useful to occasionally hold open meetings
   that AA members are invited to attend. This will forward mutual understanding and cooperation.[84]

---

80. See the *Al-Anon/Alateen Service Manual*, "Groups at Work" section, Meeting
    Ideas.
81. The Serenity Prayer was formerly referred to as The AA Prayer.
82. Al-Anon's monthly magazine is now called *The Forum*.
83. See Policy Digest, Outside Publications section in *Al-Anon/Alateen Service
    Manual*.
84. In May 1973 the Suggested Closing was added to the text for the first time.
    See Appendix II, #19 for the text.

Part II—Traditions[85]

The Twelve Traditions of the Al-Anon Family Groups tell how the groups are related to AA, to each other and to the headquarters. They describe how the movement handles questions of money, property, public relations and anonymity. The Traditions are an over-all guide for unity and function, regarded by most members as indispensable for the survival of our Society.

Al-Anon Traditions[86]

Our group experience suggests that the unity of the Al-Anon Family Groups depends upon our adherence to these Traditions:

1. Our common welfare should come first; personal progress for the greatest number depends upon unity.

2. For our group purpose there is but one authority—a loving God as He may express Himself in our group conscience. Our leaders are but trusted servants—they do not govern.

3. The only requirement for membership is that there be a problem of alcoholism in a relative or friend. The relatives of alcoholics, when gathered together for mutual aid, may call themselves an Al-Anon Family Group, provided that, as a group, they have no other affiliation.

4. Each group should be autonomous, except in matters affecting other Al-Anon Family Groups, or AA as a whole.[87]

---

85. The Traditions as printed here predate ratification by the World Service Conference in 1961. Numerous revisions were made from 1955 to 1961, and the differences are described in the identified footnotes.

86. Prior to the first World Service Conference in 1961, Lois did not make any changes to the Traditions arbitrarily. She wrote to existing Al-Anon groups and to many AA groups for their suggestions. Some of their responses are in the WSO archives. The Conference ratified the Traditions in 1961 as they were adapted.

87. The current wording as adopted in 1961: "Each group should be autonomous, except in matters affecting another group or Al-Anon or AA as a whole."

5. Each Al-Anon Family Group has but one purpose: to help families of alcoholics. We do this by practicing the Twelve Steps of AA *ourselves*, by encouraging and understanding our alcoholic relatives, and by welcoming and giving comfort to families of alcoholics.

6. Our Family Groups ought never to endorse, finance or lend our name to any outside enterprise, lest problems of money, property and prestige divert us from our primary spiritual aim; but although a separate entity, we should always cooperate with Alcoholics Anonymous.[88]

7. Every group ought to be fully self-supporting, declining outside contributions.

8. Al-Anon Twelfth-Step work should remain forever non-professional, but our service centers may employ special workers.

9. Our groups, as such, ought never be organized; but we may create service boards or committees directly responsible to those they serve.

10. The Al-Anon Family Groups have no opinion on outside issues; hence our name ought never be drawn into public controversy.

11. Our public relations policy is based on attraction rather than promotion; we need always maintain personal anonymity at the level of press, radio, and films. We need guard with special care the anonymity of all AA members.[89]

12. Anonymity is the spiritual foundation of all our Traditions, ever reminding us to place principles above personalities.

---

88. With the 1960 revised printing, this Tradition was presented with the wording as it is known today: " ...spiritual aim. Although a separate entity, we should always cooperate with Alcoholics Anonymous."

89. TV was added to this Tradition in 1960.

Part III—Group Structure[90]

The organization of an Al-Anon Family Group is very simple, but it has to have enough form to avoid confusion. Even a small group needs a program chairman and secretary. The secretary can act as treasurer as well, until the group is large enough to need a separate treasurer. As the group grows, a Service or Advisory committee is useful. Some groups also have a refreshment chairman. All officers and committees are on a rotating basis, elected by a business meeting held every three or six months, and usually called before or after a regular meeting.

The Program Chairman of a group plans the meetings in advance and obtains speakers. She either leads the meeting herself or appoints a leader.

Where there are enough Al-Anon groups in an area to warrant an Intergroup Association (some places call this a Central Office or United Council),[91] the Program Chairmen meets regularly with other Program Chairmen[92] of the area and arranges "Exchange meetings,"[93] where a team from one group conducts the meetings for a neighboring group. In this way the scope of the group is broadened and a schedule of meeting program can be planned well in advance.

The Secretary is the link between the Clearing House and the group. She receives all Headquarters bulletins as well as the monthly *Forum* and sees that every member has a chance to read them.

She keeps an up-to-date list of names, addresses and telephone numbers of all members and sees that they are notified about meetings.

She orders sufficient Al-Anon literature, not only for the group's use but enough to hand out to guests, to ministers, doctors and welfare workers.

---

90. This title was later changed to "Suggested Group Structure."

91. Today this is known as an Al-Anon information service (AIS) or intergroup.

92. See Al-Anon & Alateen Groups at Work, Group Structure section in the *Al-Anon/Alateen Service Manual*.

93. See Policy Digest, Local Service, Information Services (Intergroup) section in the *Al-Anon/Alateen Service Manual*.

She see to it that the literature is on display at meetings.

During the intermission, at the time the contribution basket is being passed at the meeting, she makes whatever announcements there may be.

The Treasurer, of course, has the custody and disbursing of whatever money there is. Family Groups do not need much, but sufficient to cover the rent and perhaps light and heat of a meeting; spring and fall contributions[94] to the Clearing House to help carry on Al-Anon work through the world, and for literature. There may be a few miscellaneous expenses, such as the cost of an announcement in the paper or a PO Box. Many groups also serve light refreshments after each meeting. In areas where there is an Intergroup, the local groups contribute towards its operating costs.

The treasurer, of course, keeps a record of all receipts and expenditures and makes a complete report of the group's financial status at each business meeting, held periodically, usually either before or after the regular meeting.

Budgeting group expenses will help simplify bookkeeping and give some ideas of the funds needed by the group. In addition to the contribution basket usually passed at meetings during the intermission, some groups augment their intake with pledges from older members who desire to make them.

Most groups find that having more money than they actually need is an unnecessary burden and even sometimes causes friction about how to spend it.

A Service or Advisory Committee composed of the officers and perhaps several older members is useful to handle questions of policy, local public relations, intergroup relations, and any internal problems that may come along.

---

94. Since 1998 these have been known as "quarterly appeals" mailed directly to the groups for individual member contributions to the World Service Office.

Part IV—Family Group Literature[95][96]

(Price list will be sent upon request.)

Books

THE AL-ANON FAMILY GROUPS (This Handbook)

ALCOHOLICS ANONYMOUS (The AA Book of Experience)[97]

THE TWELVE STEPS AND THE TWELVE TRADITIONS (Interpretive and Inspirational AA Material)

PRIMER ON ALCOHOLISM (by Marty Mann)

Monthly Periodicals

FAMILY GROUP FORUM (Newsletter, One Copy Free to Each Group[98]

THE AA GRAPEVINE

Pamphlets

THE ALCOHOLIC WIFE[99]

THE ALCOHOLIC HUSBAND[100]

ALCOHOLISM, THE FAMILY DISEASE (Help and personal stories for wives)

ALCOHOLISM AND YOU (Reprint from *Pageant Magazine*)

WORLD FAMILY GROUP DIRECTORY (One copy free annually to each Group)[101]

---

95. This listing of specific literature was deleted with the second printing in 1956. See Appendix II, #20 for the replacement wording.

96. See Appendix II, #21 on the development of the Al-Anon Conference Approved Literature process.

97. See Appendix II, #22 for an explanation on the use of AA literature in the early days.

98. The mailing of one free copy of *The Forum* to each registered Al-Anon group was discontinued in October 1978, as it was no longer financially feasible.

99. This pamphlet was discontinued.

100. This pamphlet was discontinued.

101. This directory was discontinued in 1988. Newcomers and members can call toll-free 1-888-4AL-ANON for meeting information.

Leaflets

PURPOSES AND SUGGESTIONS (Introduction to Family Groups)[102]

SUGGESTED PROGRAM (Types of Meetings)

GROUP STRUCTURE (For the New Group)

HOW TO START A GROUP

FAMILY GROUP TRADITIONS (Basic Principles for Group Survival)

SUGGESTED WELCOME AND PREAMBLE TO THE TWELVE STEPS

NEW HELP FOR ALCOHOLICS (Reprint from *Coronet Magazine*)

ONE WIFE'S STORY (By the Wife of an Early AA)

HOW ONE AA WIFE LIVES THE TWELVE STEPS (Reprint from the *AA Grapevine*)

FREEDOM FROM DESPAIR (Adapted from a local Family Group pamphlet)

YOU CAN HELP AN ALCOHOLIC (Reprint from the *Christian Herald*)

Purse or Wallet Card

JUST FOR TODAY

Family Stories in "The AA Grapevine"

"The AA Grapevine" is the monthly publication of Alcoholics Anonymous, published at General Service Headquarters of AA. It contains informative and inspirational material by and for AA members and others interested in the problem of alcoholism. It has published a number of articles of interest to relatives and friends of alcoholics. Special prices prevail for issues more than two years old.

---

102. The title was changed to *Purpose and Suggestions* in 1976, when the WSO Policy Committee affirmed that Al-Anon has but one purpose: To help families and friends of alcoholics.

The issues of October, 1946, August, 1947 and September, 1951, are no longer available. The address of "*The AA Grapevine*" is 241 East Broadway, New York, 2, N.Y.[103][104]

Dec.	1944	Bill's wife remembers when he and she and AA were young.
		A Father Looks Through His Son's Eyes.
		The Children Say What AA Means To Them.
		Time On Our Hands.
May	1945	A Wife Takes Pleasure in AA.
		A Daughter is Proud of Her Mother.
		Credo of an AA Wife.
Feb.	1946	Are Families People?
Mar.	1946	Tribute from Son.
		Mail Call—One Wife's Views.
		Another Wife's Views.
Apr.	1946	A Word to the Wise (Wives).
Aug.	1946	God Made our Relatives, Too.
Oct.	1946	Marital Readjustments Necessary.
Nov.	1946	An Alcoholic's Wife Finds Many Ways to Help.
Dec.	1946	Are AA Women and Wives Smug?
Jan.	1947	Wives Need Understanding.
Feb.	1947	A Word to the Wise AA Parent.
Mar.	1947	Our Children, Too, Appreciate What AA Has Given Us.
		AA Book Encourages Wife (about slips).
Apr.	1947	Husband Sees Rich Reward for Non-alcoholics.
May	1947	Family Groups make Headway in California.
Aug.	1947	Wives Can Well Follow AA's Example.
Nov.	1947	Frisco Family Group Sums up Purposes.

---

103. The AA address is now PO Box 1980, Grand Central Station, New York, NY 10163-1980.

104. These articles are no longer available from AA.

Dec. 1947   A Wife Learns How Best to Really Help.
Mar. 1948   AA Contacts Help Wives in Comeback.
Apr. 1948   Wives are People, Too.
July 1948   N.A.A. organized in Rochester.
Aug. 1948   A Son Speaks about AA.
             Families, Wives Need Help, Too, and Can Gain
             from the Twelve Steps.
Sept. 1948   Let's Give the Non-alcoholic Wife a Break.
Dec. 1948   Your Wife May Be Sick, Too.
May   1949   I Am a Proud Wife.
June 1949   From One Mother to Another.
Aug. 1949   "Don'ts" for the Non-alcoholic.
Feb. 1950   Helpful Household Hints.
             It Might Have Been the Time.
Feb. 1950   Advice to the Three Wives.
Mar. 1950   Advice to the Three Wives.
July 1950   The Non-alcoholic—God Bless 'em.
Oct. 1950   Every Family Club Member Knows the Story.
Nov. 1950   The Arena.
Apr. 1951   From a Wife Who Never Understood.
June 1951   The Non-alcoholic Wife's Quandary.
Aug. 1951   AA Associates.
             Keep the Slate Clean.
Sept. 1951   Chicago Wives.
Mar. 1952   A Non-AA on Prayer.
             Encouragement for New Members' Wives.
Apr. 1952   PO Box 1475.
Nov. 1952   I am Confused.
             Report from the Hearthside Family Group
             Traditions.

July   1953   Family Circle—The Voice of the Tadpole.
                Love in Bloom?
Aug.   1953   I Stayed for the Sake of the Children.
                Family Circle—How One AA Wife Lives the
                Twelve Steps.
                It Takes Two.
Sept.   1953   Family Circle—As Non-alcoholic Mates and
                Families See the AA Program.
Oct.   1953   Family Circle—As Non-alcoholic Mates and
                Families See the AA Program.
Dec.   1953   Our Merriest Christmas.
Jan.   1954   I Learned My Dad Was Sick.
                It's Not Fair.
Feb.   1954   The Wife and the AA Program.
Mar.   1954   A Daughter Thinks.
May   1954   Family Circle—A Daughter's Story.
June   1954   A Letter from an AA Father to his Son.
July   1954   It's Not Fair (An answer to Jan. 1954).
Sept.   1954   How Did We Get There?
                A Grateful Parent.
                Al-Anons for "Nons."
Nov.   1954   Then and Now.

APPENDIX II

Appendix II provides readers with additional historical documentation and information on the development of the Al-Anon program. The year 2000 brings a promise of hope for Al-Anon's future as well as an opportunity to celebrate the past. Over the years wording changes have been made in statements that are commonly heard and read by members. Documentation of the changes was not always retained, so we don't always know the "whys." Trusting in the Al-Anon Conference Approved Literature process was essential in our early days just as it is today. This appendix provides us with a unique glimpse into Al-Anon's past.

TABLE OF CONTENTS TO APPENDIX II

Other additions to the book in subsequent editions:

1. Revised Note from 1960 Edition

"This book is designed to be helpful to all those who live with an alcoholic. It is hoped, also, that it will shed some light on the subject of alcoholism as it affects not only the relatives and friends of problem drinkers but those who come in daily contact, professionally and socially, with alcoholics."

2. 1960 Revised Introduction and the Serenity Prayer

Throughout the first edition, the Serenity Prayer is referred to as "the AA prayer." In 1960 the Serenity Prayer was added to the introduction of the book. It is interesting to note that with this first printing it was incorrectly presented in the text:

Introduction

"The Al-Anon Family Groups are a fellowship of wives, husbands, relatives and friends of members of Alcoholics Anonymous and of problem drinkers generally. Members of Al-Anon are banded together to solve their common problems of fear, insecurity, lack of understanding of the alcoholic, and of the warped family relationships associated with alcoholism.

"The message of Al-Anon Family Groups is a story of hope. It is the story of men and women who once felt helpless and powerless to deal with the alcoholism of their loved ones. Today these men and women no longer feel lost or lonely. They have learned that there are simple things they can do directly to help themselves and indirectly to help their alcoholic partners.

"Many who are now members of Family Groups have already seen their loved ones achieve sobriety, but they have found that life with a sober alcoholic can present special problems of adjustment. Others still have active problem drinkers in their homes. All of them need the fellowship which Al-Anon affords. All of them find strength and comfort in one of Al-Anon's tenets,   the Serenity Prayer:[105]   God grant me the serenity
              to accept the things I cannot change,
              the courage to change the things I can
              and the wisdom to know the difference."

3. Adoption of the Twelve Traditions

In 1958 Lois asked that the following paragraph be added to the upcoming revision. It was edited in later editions.

"At the request of the groups for some sort of unified pattern upon which group action could be based, the Twelve Traditions of AA were adapted to our own use.[106] These principles were accepted throughout the Al-Anon Family Groups as a framework within which the groups could function in unity. They became as important a guide to the groups as the Twelve Steps were to the individual."

4. Trustees

The following are definitions which come from the *Al-Anon/ Alateen Service Manual* to assist readers in understanding the differences in election procedures.

---

105. The underlined words are incorrect.
106. The Twelve Traditions were adopted in 1952.

Board of Trustees: "The Board of Trustees is comprised of seven to twenty-one members: one sustaining member (the Executive Director), trustees-at-large, and regional trustees. Our co-founders Lois W. and Anne B., now deceased, were honorary lifetime members. The term of office for both trustees-at-large and regional trustees is three years; they may serve [a maximum of] two terms, which may be consecutive."

Trustee-at-large: Candidates submit qualifying resumes to the World Service Office. Nominees are interviewed and selected by the full Board of Trustees and their selection is given traditional approval at the following World Service Conference.

Regional Trustee: Candidates submit qualifying resumes and are nominated by their respective areas. The nominee is selected by members of the regional nominating committee and at-large members from other regions at the World Service Conference.[107]

5. Is Al-Anon For You?[108]

"Go to any typical Al-Anon Group and you will find a cross section of many kinds of people. They differ so much as to age, occupation, background and temperament that they offer each other a rich and varied experience in friendship. The vital things they have in common are a compulsive drinker in their immediate or past lives and a sincere desire to do something constructive about the situation.

"Because there are more men than women alcoholics, almost all Al-Anon Groups have a preponderance of women members. Afternoon meetings may be composed almost entirely of women, but evening meetings include a good many husbands and some fathers and sons of alcoholics. Several groups have already gone completely stag. Most groups welcome the fuller view of the family dilemma which a mixed membership provides.

---

107. For additional information on trustees, see the *Al-Anon/Alateen Service Manual* or write to the World Service Office.

108. This chapter was added in 1960.

"Since Al-Anon has its roots in Alcoholics Anonymous and is closely associated with it, many Al-Anon members have alcoholic relatives in AA, some of whom have achieved sobriety, while others are still having trouble.

"In recent years, furthermore, a growing number of social agencies, alcoholic centers and clinics, individual doctors, ministers, and judges are referring relatives of alcoholics to Al-Anon as a source of help in rebuilding their own troubled lives. The increased amount of information on alcoholism that reaches the public through the press, radio and television also greatly enlarges the number of relatives of alcoholics who hear about Al-Anon. The message is getting across that Al-Anon's primary purpose is not to try to stop the alcoholic's drinking but to help his family lead a saner, happier and more effective life.

"This increased general knowledge of alcoholism fortunately brings many people into Al-Anon at early stages of the alcoholic problem. A generation ago wives and husbands of alcoholics struggled for years through their dreary and sometimes dangerous lives without help. Today thousands of relatives of compulsive drinkers are seeking aid before drinking has ruined home life beyond repair or taken too heavy a toll on the sanity and health of their non-alcoholic. Not only partners but also adolescent children of alcoholics are learning in increased numbers that they, too, can find comfort and some sense of security through the therapy that shared experience with a group affords.

"Here, then, are the three kinds of people you will find in Al-Anon:

1. The wife (or husband, or other relative) of an AA member who is leading a consistently sober life.

2. The relative of an AA member who is still having trouble with drinking.

3. The relative of an alcoholic who refuses help from AA or any other source.

"Among the first group you will find some women whose personality and thinking have been so warped by years of confusion that they need help even after their partners have been sober for some time. Others, having rebuilt their own lives with Al-Anon's help, continue to want the inspiration of the group or are so grateful that they attend meetings in an effort to help new members.

"It is easy to understand why people in the second and third classifications seek Al-Anon's help. Since AA has benefited the alcoholic in spite of relapses, there is good reason to hope that the family's greater understanding of the problem may lead to firmer adherence to the Twelve Steps on the part of the alcoholic. And certainly the relative of an active alcoholic needs the program of Al-Anon desperately."

In 1974, the "three kinds of people" were rewritten, the fourth "kind" was added, and the introduction was revised to read:

"Among Al-Anon and Alateen members you will find in the fellowship are the relatives or close friends of:

1. an AA member who is leading a consistently sober life.

2. an alcoholic who is trying to overcome his compulsion, but is still suffering sporadic lapses.

3. an alcoholic who refuses help from any source.

4. an alcoholic who is separated from his family or has died.

"Among the first group you will find some women whose personality and thinking have been so warped by years of confusion that they need help even after their partners have been sober for some time. Others, having rebuilt their own lives with Al-Anon's help, continue to want the inspiration of the group or are so grateful that they attend meetings in an effort to help new members.

"People in the second classification need Al-Anon to help them maintain strength to meet the disappointment and frustration of the alcoholic's lapses from sobriety. As they grow in understanding of the problem in Al-Anon, there is good reason to hope that their improved attitudes will finally bring the wavering AA member to solid sobriety.

"The family of the alcoholic obviously needs Al-Anon in order to learn how to live with the confusions and despairs created by an active drinking problem. For in Al-Anon they gain confidence that few cases are hopeless. Even the most stubborn refusal to seek help often changes to acceptance once the family's attitude has changed for the better.

"Even when the alcoholic no longer is an active member of the family because of either separation or death, those whose lives have been deeply affected by close contact with a problem drinker continue to feel a need for the comfort, support and encouragement of the group. Adult children of alcoholics find that, although they may no longer live with an alcoholic parent, their lives have been affected and Al-Anon can help them in many ways."

6. After Sobriety

The following paragraphs were added to the text in March 1960.

"When our husbands or wives first join Alcoholics Anonymous, many of them undergo a miraculous change, and life seems very rosy indeed. What we have hoped and vainly striven for through the years has now become a reality. For a few of us the bright prospect never dims, but for many of us it turns out otherwise. We still feel vaguely insecure. We lack serenity for today and confidence for tomorrow. We quarrel over trifles. We find that the process of adjusting to our partner's new way of life in AA brings a fresh set of difficulties, problems which must be solved if a happy home life is to be recreated.

"We find that when we ourselves attend open meetings of AA we begin to change our perspective. We notice first of all that the AA program usually results in a profound change in thinking and everyday behavior of sober alcoholics. This change, affecting the entire personality of the alcoholic, seems to come about as a result of an honest and searching personal inventory of his own faults.

"Another thing we notice is that when we non-alcoholics talk with one another and exchange ideas, we are able to apply another's experience to our own particular problems. As non-alcoholic partners, we discover that we have as much to gain through AA's suggested Twelve Steps of recovery as the alcoholics do. We find that alcoholism has made us sick too, and that we need emotional sobriety as much as our alcoholics need freedom from alcohol. When we begin to examine our own attitudes, we are amazed to see how warped our thinking has become.

"After a period of sobriety our recovered alcoholics become qualified to resume responsibilities, but we are not always willing to let them do so. Running things our own way has become a deeply ingrained habit. As a result, when our partners attempt to resume duties which are rightfully theirs, they often encounter direct or indirect resistance from us, and tensions develop which might have been avoided through an Easy Does It attitude.

"Little by little we come nearer to being honest with ourselves. Some of us begin to realize, for example, that many of our defects have little relation to our partner's alcoholism. Or it may be that we are still harboring resentments, unconsciously rebelling against the burdens of the past. Perhaps we resent the fact that someone or something other than ourselves has been able to help our partner to stop drinking. We are faced with the change from being an important prop in our alcoholic's life to becoming a mere incidental in his recovery at the hands of others. This would present a challenge to even well-adjusted minds, and ours are far from that.

"Some of us are not above bemoaning the fact that a newly sober husband now labors long and diligently to make up for lost time in his business affairs. Sometimes we even resent the time that our sober alcoholics spend at AA meetings or in working with alcoholics who are still drinking. In time we come to realize that what we felt previously was possessiveness and not true partnership.

"Even though we eventually learn to release our partners to their business lives and AA activities, we still may feel isolated and lonely. We know that our alcoholics, regardless of family ties, felt themselves to be the loneliest persons in the world before they found Alcoholics Anonymous. This is a clue to the way out of our own personal dilemma of loneliness. After the first breathtaking feeling of relief and release from tensions when our alcoholics have finally accepted AA, we find ourselves standing alone once more amid the wreckage which alcoholism leaves in the wake. We look about us and see that the recovered alcoholics ease their burdens by sharing their experience and problems with others who understand them. Since this sharing is helpful to alcoholics, might it not benefit their non-alcoholic partners as well?

"In the Al-Anon Family Groups we have found that it does just that. Similarly, those of us whose alcoholics still refuse help through AA or other means are inspired by Al-Anon's way of life. Although still harassed by an active drinking problem, we find it possible to arrange our own lives more confidently and to create a better emotional climate in our homes. At first we may feel that the Twelve Steps do not apply to us. Gradually, however, we realize that our needs, too, are adequately fulfilled by application of their spiritual depth and wisdom."

7. The Twelve Steps

A chapter on the Twelve Steps was added in the 1960 revision with the following:

"We need Al-Anon and the people in Al-Anon to help us apply the precepts of the Twelve Steps to our complicated lives in specific ways. We cannot assimilate these principles overnight, or in a week, a month, or even a year. They must be taken slowly and easily.

"Each one is free, of course, to choose his or her own order in which to follow the Twelve Steps. Many of us, however, feel that by working the Steps one by one in the order in which they have been set down, we reach a fuller understanding of what they can do for us.

"Step One

We admitted we were powerless over alcohol—that our lives had become unmanageable.

"The First Step is the platform upon which all the others are based. Until we are convinced, emotionally as well as intellectually, that we are powerless over alcohol and its effects on our alcoholics, we will run into trouble and will be unable to make progress with the rest of the Steps.

"When our lives become uncontrollable, we usually feel that it is the fault of our alcoholics alone, but that they will eventually stop drinking because they love us. We may not yet know that we are dealing with a mighty compulsion which has become complete master of them and allows no interference. We may try being strong, weak, firm, cajoling, angry, loving and tender—or we may use the silent treatment—only to find that no approach is successful. We accomplish nothing but an added confusion, our own frustration, and the loss of hope and trust. If we still retain a lurking hope that love or fear or anything else—except the alcoholic's own desire for sobriety—will keep him from drinking, we have not fully accepted the fact that we have no power over this compulsion.

"The simple admission that we are powerless, if made with conviction, may bring its own reward. With full acceptance that no one can help the alcoholic until he is ready and willing to do something about it himself, there comes a profound feeling of release. We then find that we can turn our attention toward managing our own lives in a more orderly fashion. This accomplished, the home atmosphere becomes more peaceful, and spiritual growth can follow.

"There have been many concrete examples to prove that a change in our attitude has resulted in helping alcoholics to stop, think, and eventually seek help for themselves. This has happened too often to be explained as coincidental, and it can happen to us if we take this First Step seriously and follow with the other Steps."

"Step Two

Came to believe that a Power greater than ourselves could restore us to sanity.

"Many of us have despaired of receiving help from any source. If we had spiritual resources at one time they seem to have ebbed with each disappointment, with each broken promise. But when we admit our own powerlessness and our dependence on a Higher Power, hope is reawakened. We overcome fear by renewing or finding faith in a God, who, to all appearances, seemed to have deserted us or to have been non-existent. After accepting the mere possibility of a Greater Power, we come to believe more and more strongly that we can rely on this Power to help us, if we ourselves are willing to cooperate.

"We still may retain vague fears for the future, but we learn to banish unnamed terrors by trying to live a day at a time and being willing to accept what we cannot change. When this is done, things have a way of straightening themselves out without our interference.

"There are other things that we can do. For instance, if our fear is for our children and effects of alcoholism on them, we can reduce this fear by working toward a healthy emotional atmosphere in the home, with the help of Al-Anon.

"If we fear financial insecurity resulting from the irresponsibility of the head of the house, we may find a solution by taking a job ourselves, by changing our general attitude toward this victim of a disease, and by placing our trust in God.

"Step Three

Made a decision to turn our will and our lives over to the care of God as we understood Him.

"Certain newcomers attend Al-Anon meetings because they are desperate, but their minds are closed. They expect sympathy and when they see that they are not getting the kind they want, they lose interest. They may have read that alcoholism is a disease, one which they are powerless to curb or cure, but they think their case is different. They have not really accepted the basic facts of their situation. All that is needed, however, is an open mind. If they can be persuaded to continue to come to meetings, they will observe that others, many of whom have faced the same or worse problems, have obviously been helped.

"Gradually it becomes apparent to the newcomers that the more serene members have not only admitted their powerlessness, but have surrendered their decisions and their lives. No one in Al-Anon asks the extent of your faith. It remains a wholly personal commitment to God as the individual understands Him. Spiritual surrender, however, may come sooner and have deeper roots through the warmth and contagion of Al-Anon's fellowship.

"Step Four

Made a searching and fearless moral inventory of ourselves.

"Our self-respect is somewhat restored by taking the first three Steps. We are relieved of feelings of inadequacy and shame. And now our increasing desire for peace of mind and spiritual growth leaves no alternative but to do something about our character defects, especially those we had even before a drinking problem entered our lives.

"In taking personal inventory, assets as well as liabilities should be considered. If we did not have some virtues along with our faults, we would not be able to take the Fourth Step successfully. It would be too painful. We would indeed not be able to attempt the work of this program at all without possessing *some* virtue.

"Approaching Step Four, we have already admitted powerlessness, professed submissiveness, and placed reliance on a Higher Power as we understand it. Now complete honesty is required in order to know ourselves.

"Thoroughness, therefore, ought to be our watchword when taking inventory. It is wise to write out our questions and answers. This is an aid to clear thinking and honest appraisal. It is the first *tangible* evidence of our complete willingness to move forward.

"The program suggests twenty-four-hour living. In order to live peaceably in the present, however, we must rid ourselves of the ghosts of past guilt feelings. They must be recognized for what they are and flushed out. Only then can they be permanently dispelled. If kept deep within and unnoticed, they may influence our whole lives without our realizing it; if they become too deeply ingrained, serious complications may develop.

"How else can we know ourselves except through searching inventories? It is slow and painstaking work, but when it is begun many things fall into place and we are encouraged to continue. The sooner we feel able to attempt this Step and the more thoroughly we take it, the greater will be the relief and the sooner will we start growing.

"Step Five

Admitted to God, to ourselves, and to another human being the exact nature of our wrongs.

"Hidden guilts and subtle character defects have been ignored or rationalized or consciously buried so far back in our memories that we have almost forgotten them. These cause much of the trouble in any human being, whether confronted by alcoholism or not. It is not easy to dig out faults which we prefer to dismiss from our minds. It is difficult to face them conscientiously and to admit them to God and to ourselves. But it is still harder to admit them to another human being, whether confronted by alcoholism or not.

"It is not easy to dig out faults which we prefer to dismiss from our minds. It is difficult to face them conscientiously and to admit them to God and to ourselves. But it is still harder to admit them to another human being. Experience has taught us, however, that another person with an objective viewpoint can not only provide essential help in this assessment, but can also help us to forgive ourselves. When we openly admit our resentments, our self-pity, and our other harmful states, we have taken a big step toward banishing them.

"Step Six

Were entirely ready to have God remove all these defects of character.

"Our experience also has shown us that we can make little progress in removing our defects without help from a Higher Power. Step Six is a good place to pause, review the progress we have made, and try to strengthen our contact with God in order to gain His grace in the removal of our defects.

"It is not good enough to see that we have faults and merely make vague resolutions to do better. We must co-operate sincerely in their elimination. A good way to get results is to concentrate on a single defect and work on it alone for a while. As continued effort meets with some success in reducing one or two faults, we gain courage to attack more serious defects. We must be honest with ourselves about our willingness to let God remove them all. Some of us have discovered that we have certain pet vices which we recognize but are not yet ready to give up. Strange as it may seem, the mere willingness to accept the help of God often brings us strength to move forward in this vital work on ourselves.

"Step Seven

Humbly asked Him to remove our shortcomings.

"In the preceding Step it was suggested that we become willing to have God remove our faults. In this Step we humbly ask Him to do so. The whole emphasis here is on humility, a quality which consists not of servility but of seeing ourselves in true perspective—in relation to our alcoholic partner, to our fellowmen, and to God. Hence we humbly ask Him to remove shortcomings which alone we find impossible to cope with.

"Step Eight

Made a list of all persons we had harmed and became willing to make amends to them all.

"After the searching inventory and truth-facing required in Steps Four through Seven, it is not difficult to remember the persons we have harmed over the years. Foremost, of course, is our alcoholic. Before we realized the nature of his disease, we often berated him for his behavior when drunk and his irresponsibility when sober. When we are able to turn our lives over to a Power greater than ourselves, we lose the inclination to punish our partner and to dwell on our own years of suffering. Indeed, we get glimpses of how much *he* may have suffered from our martyr-like attitude or our criticism and nagging. Willingness to make amends to our alcoholic gives new meaning to the serenity prayer; at last we seem able to have gained 'the courage to change the things we can.'

"This same open-mindedness applies to our attitude toward our children. We begin to recall all the times when anxiety and despair made us short and unreasonable in our dealings with them. We are newly aware of the fact that when they sometimes sympathized with their alcoholic parent, we resented it bitterly. We become willing to make amends as soon and generously as possible.

"Hurt by the criticism of in-laws and other relatives, we often leapt angrily to the defense of our mates, or retaliated by pointing out our critics' faults or those of their associates and relatives. We add these names to the list of the injured.

"Certain friends had been brushed off coldly or more openly resented, although they might have been sincerely understanding at the time. And some of us were guilty of impatience and intolerance of even the doctors and clergymen who tried to help us. Instead of recognizing that the best professional people can do little if the alcoholic refuses to admit his problem, in our bewilderment and ignorance we accused our counselors of misunderstanding or stupidity. We remember them all in naming those to whom apology and amends are due.

"Step Nine

Made direct amends to such people wherever possible, except when to do so would injure them or others.

"This Step should be very carefully considered. As non-alcoholics, we seldom inflicted physical injury, but were guilty of causing mental, emotional, and even spiritual pain to others. We cannot right old wrongs by thoughtlessly adverting to the original injury or by carelessly involving other persons in present difficulties. We must manage to make constructive amends.

"Even in making amends to the alcoholic with whom we live, we must weigh carefully the desirability of mentioning old injustices. Often it is kinder and more fruitful to bury the past in a decent silence and show our regret by a loving and understanding present attitude. Lightening the daily atmosphere with cheer and hope may do more for many alcoholics than reviving old scenes, even though we take the blame for part of them. This applies also to the children, in-laws and other relatives.

"If, however, apologies seem in order to clear the way for a warmer understanding, we should make them freely, not allowing ourselves to rationalize in order to get out of an unpleasant task. When we have made personal amends generously and with care not to hurt anyone, we do indeed enjoy a great sense of relief and take a major step in character growth.

"Step Ten

Continued to take personal inventory and when we were wrong promptly admitted it.

"To take any of the Steps just once is never enough. Emphasis here is placed on taking repeated inventory, since many of us have not yet acquired the habit of accurate self-appraisal. If we can make inventories a part of our everyday living and acquire the habit of taking one each night, we can be assured that we are making great strides toward continuing peace of mind and growth.

"There is a spiritual axiom which says that every time we are disturbed, no matter what the cause, there is something wrong with US. When someone hurts us and we become angry, WE, too, are in the wrong. A quick summing up at the time the situation arises can save us a lot of grief then and eliminate an item from future inventories. If we thoughtlessly or angrily injure someone, immediate apology saves hours of unnecessary suffering for both participants.

"Old faults have a way of creeping back from time to time in different guises. Sometimes resentments persist an incredible length of time and actually seem to grow in intensity if we give them lodging in our minds. At the moment of discovery and admission, therefore, we must acknowledge these thoughts as poisonous ones and firmly deny them our consent.

"Step Eleven

Sought through prayer and meditation to improve our conscious contract with God as we understood Him, praying only for knowledge of His will for us and the power to carry that out.

"When we pray or meditate we often see things in a new light, sometimes dramatically so, making us feel sure that God as we understand Him is near. We see this mostly in retrospect, since we are often too blind to recognize simple truths when they occur. A common instance is when we find we have prayed for something we thought was good, only to have it turn out to be the worst thing possible for us.

"If we pray only for the knowledge of God's will for us, we simply cannot go wrong. We whose lives have revolved about the disease of alcoholism have seen miracles of sobriety accomplished. Most of us feel that this is not just coincidence; it has happened through the grace of God and AA. There are too many things that point toward divine help to ignore or deny it.

"Many of us who had despaired of believing in any God, or in almost anything for that matter, have eventually renewed our faith or found a new one through following these Steps.

"Step Twelve

Having had a spiritual awakening as the result of these steps, we tried to carry this message to others and to practice these principles in all our affairs.

"Spiritual awakenings need not come with great fanfare. It may occur simply and quietly through full acceptance of the principles of the Twelve Steps and a sincere attempt to practice them. It is not at all necessary for us to wait for a revelation before trying to help others, before trying to carry the message.

"The real and abiding proof that these principles have actually become part of our lives comes when we, having adopted these

Steps and having started to grow spiritually, open our hearts unstintingly to those who are still burdened.

"Many people come to Al-Anon who have had, and may still have, deep religious faith. To them, living by the Twelve Steps amplifies a daily contact with the Higher Power on whom they have always relied.

"Others without formal or religious beliefs often find that the Twelve Steps become a spiritual way of life in themselves. Faith sometimes comes even to those who rebel and say, 'There is no God.' If these rebellious ones stay around long enough to take the First Step and DO some of the things suggested in the other Steps, a great change may come over them and faith creep in almost unnoticed.

"There are some, however, who have a spiritual 'awakening' in a very literal sense of the term, and this can happen to any of us, regardless of religious status or lack of it. After such an experience, these people are able to see, feel, and believe with a conviction of which they were previously incapable. A sudden insight may appear as an utterly new approach toward the solution of a grave problem. This awakening brings with it greatly enlarged capacities for honesty, unselfishness, and love in all departments of daily living. There is access to a new source of understanding and strength. These persons have been placed, through no effort of their own except co-operation and willingness, on a new plane of consciousness which they know will be lasting.

"It is a lifetime job to apply the Steps to our everyday lives. In trying to practice the Twelfth Step work, we can help new members by telling our story at meetings and identifying our experience with theirs. By going along with our partner when he visits a new prospect, we can give comfort to the wives and encourage her to go to Al-Anon meetings.

"It may be helpful to make it clear that Twelfth Step work in Al-Anon should be directed only to Al-Anon members or other non-alcoholics. Much as we may want to carry the message to alcoholics, whether in AA or not, we are not equipped to do so any more than they, the alcoholics, can help us with our particular problems as relatives of problem drinkers.

"We can help members of our group in periods of particular stress by a phone call or visit. We can give of our time and understanding whenever the opportunity presents, not only to Al-Anon members but to all with whom we come in contact."[109]

8. The Twelve Traditions[110]

"Al-Anon's Twelve Traditions are guides for the conduct and unity of the groups, just as the Twelve Steps are guides for the lives and growth of individual members. Since Al-Anon has no rules or regulations, the Traditions form a framework of common consent within which we may best carry on our activities. By following these traditional principles, groups can avoid many of the pitfalls into which the early membership fell. For the Traditions tell how the groups are related to each other and to Al-Anon and AA as a whole.

"The Traditions also indicate desirable attitudes toward membership, group purposes, money, property, public relations, leadership, and anonymity. These principles are only suggestions which no group is compelled to observe. The unity of the Al-Anon fellowship, however, and perhaps its survival, depends upon adherence to the Traditions.

"Al-Anon is becoming increasingly Tradition-conscious. More and more groups are coming to understand the importance of the Traditions in solving everyday group problems and in continuing

---

109. The text of this section was revised numerous times over the subsequent years of publication. No wording changes have been made to the Twelve Steps.

110. This chapter was added to the book in 1960.

and extending the usefulness of Al-Anon. Most groups want to abide by these principles. A careful study and observance of them tends to prevent later heated differences of opinion."

"So let us now consider them:

"Tradition One

Our common welfare should come first; personal progress for the greatest number depends upon unity.

"Unity presents not only the necessary climate for the growth of Al-Anon as a whole but also the atmosphere in which each member within the group may acquire peace of mind.

"As one member put it, "My own emotional recovery—one of my most valued possessions, since it means sanity and well-being to me personally—depends on unity: unity at Headquarters, unity of AA and Al-Anon in my district, and unity in my own group. Last but not least, it depends upon unity and integrity within myself, in mind, body, and spirit.

"This Tradition does not imply that each member should be submerged by the group and not think, speak and act as an individual. Probably nowhere is there greater freedom of belief and action than in AA and Al-Anon. But the Tradition does imply that unless the group survives, many individuals will not recover. When this realization comes, members become willing to control their speech and actions so as not to injure other members and to make sacrifices for the preservation of the group.

"Occasionally a whole group is disrupted by an unthinking member who wants to run the group her way regardless of how others feel, or by an inconsiderate person who talks all the time, airing private feelings and grievances. The entire group thus may suffer from one member's self-indulgence—until she begins to practice Tradition One.

"Tradition Two

For our group purpose there is but one authority—a loving God as He may express Himself in our group conscience. Our leaders are but trusted servants—they do not govern.

"In Al-Anon there is an intentional absence of personal power or authority. Just as individual members turn to a Higher Power for individual guidance, so groups rely on the authority of God as expressed through the group conscience.

"Newcomers frequently ask, 'How can our fellowship function without some human authority? How does God express Himself in group conscience? And what is a group conscience anyway?'

"Since the whole purpose of Al-Anon is spiritual growth, the forms of government found in most organizations are unnecessary. Members are drawn together by their common suffering, and this identity of experience levels differences of station in life, background, education, religious or political belief, color, race, or age. No member is different from or more important than the next.

"When a group needs to solve a serious problem, it naturally becomes as well informed on the subject as possible, then discusses it from all angles. Together the members seek to be guided by a Higher Power in reaching a decision which will be good for the group as a whole rather than for any one member or clique. This decision is an expression of the group conscience, and it is usually wiser than any one leader's conclusions about the problem, especially if the leader is pressing a bit for pet ideas.

"We have leaders, but they do not exercise authority. In starting a group, older and more experienced members do unquestionably have to guide and attend to most of the chores. But once the group is established, the early leaders wisely retire to the sidelines where they can be consulted, but where they will not interfere with the principle of rotation of office. The sharing of responsibilities by all members promotes the effective development of the group conscience.

"Tradition Three

The relatives of alcoholics, when gathered together for mutual aid, may call themselves an Al-Anon Family Group, provided that, as a group, they have no other affiliation. The only requirement for membership is that there be a problem of alcoholism in a relative or friend.

"The Third Tradition gives Al-Anon an informal character and insures its singleness of purpose. If the group, as such, had other loyalties, its purpose would surely become divided.

"Anyone who has a relative or friend with an alcoholic problem may join Al-Anon simply by expressing such a desire to be a member. No one can de denied membership, no matter how grave the personal complications or past actions of the individual.

"Although the Traditions seem simple and easy to understand, questions often arise concerning membership. Can a wife belong to Al-Anon after her husband has a slip in AA? Could two wives become members, the divorced and the present wife of the same alcoholic? Should a questionable character be admitted to membership? Can the alcoholic wife of an alcoholic join Al-Anon? Can the widow of an alcoholic become an Al-Anon member? Is the mother eligible for membership if her son will not join AA?

"The same answer applies to all these questions alike. The sole qualification for membership is that the relative or friend have an alcohol problem.

"Tradition Four

Each group should be autonomous, except in matters affecting another group or Al-Anon and AA as a whole.

"Each Al-Anon group can manage its internal affairs exactly as it pleases, except when to do so might affect other groups or Al-Anon and AA as a whole. Thus, a group should not only be considerate of neighboring groups, consulting them about any proposed area activity, but should do nothing to harm the fellowships of either Al-Anon or AA.

"When one group disregards the Traditions by indulging in idle gossip, ill-considered ballyhoo and promotion, lack of anonymity, or public solicitation of funds, the reputation of Al-Anon and even AA suffers.

"The most obvious example is the breaking of anonymity at the public level. It is easy to see what would happen if an Al-Anon group allowed itself to do this. The public would lose confidence and prospective Al-Anon members would back away, not only from this group but from other Al-Anon groups. AA, as well, would be adversely affected.

"The breaking of the other Traditions, although not as striking examples, would have similar ill results. Therefore each group has a right to be wrong, but not at the expense of other groups nor in matters that might harm the unity of the whole.

"Tradition Five

Each Al-Anon Family Group has but one purpose: to help families of alcoholics. We do this by practicing the Twelve Steps of AA ourselves, by encouraging and understanding our alcoholic relatives, and by welcoming and giving comfort to families of alcoholics.

"We cannot give away what we do not have, and so we help others by first helping ourselves. We do this by trying to practice the Twelve Steps in all our affairs. It is a lifetime job and cannot be done in one or two attempts and then set aside as an accomplished job. Relief from some of our frustrations, however, often comes immediately after a start is made. By striving to live closer and closer to these principles, we gain greater and greater peace, serenity, and usefulness to others.

"The next way we help is by learning as much as possible about the illness of alcoholism and by putting this knowledge into practice in our own homes. Going to AA meetings gives us greater understanding of the alcoholic's problem, as will reading some of the many books on the subject, particularly the basic book *Alcoholics Anonymous*. Learning how to live in some degree of peace with ourselves, even in a home where there is an active alcoholic, aids us in our demonstration to others.

"The third way we help is by enabling newcomers to realize that they are no longer alone, that we understand their problems as few can, because we have had the same or similar experiences. We recognize their need to discuss their fears and difficulties, and we encourage them to believe that their situation can be improved and their unhappiness overcome.

"As a group, we do not provide money, clothes or food, or get jobs for alcoholics' families, although individual members do as much of this as they choose. Our singleness of purpose might become divided if we entered the social welfare or charity field. Our help is educational, psychological and spiritual, given through example and understanding, and not through preachment.

"Tradition Six

Our Family Groups ought never endorse, finance or lend our name to any outside enterprise, lest problems of money, property and prestige divert us from our primary spiritual aim. Although a separate entity, we should always co-operate with Alcoholics Anonymous.

"Our lives have been so deeply affected by alcoholism that sometimes we want to attack the huge problem from every side: by supporting or running hospitals and drying out places; by changing laws about selling liquor; by preventing so much and such attractive advertising about alcohol; by putting on educational programs about its evils, etc.

"Any Al-Anon member is at perfect liberty to join these efforts if he or she chooses; but an Al-Anon group, as such, should never undertake such enterprises or lend its moral or financial support to those who do. We cannot thus divide our work, but should keep our attention focused on our own program.

"Before the importance of Tradition Six was well understood, a group wanted to do something definite about reducing the great amount of liquor advertising. They said that most of their husbands were new in AA and that so much attractive liquor advertising made it particularly hard for them to stay away from the first drink. One could go nowhere, they said, or even stay home and listen to the radio or look at television without being constantly reminded of the pleasures of drinking. These wives felt that Al-Anon as a whole should make a protest to advertising firms and liquor companies.

"When this Tradition was pointed out to them, however, they saw its reasonableness. A few of the wives, as individual citizens, did join a campaign to reduce the liquor advertising in their state, but the group, as such, did not participate in the undertaking.

"While we are a separate entity from Alcoholics Anonymous, we would not be functioning today without it. We have drawn from its experience, its Steps and its Traditions. Our meetings are held in the same manner, and the structure of our fellowships are similar. AA has generously given its help and support toward the growth of Al-Anon. We are grateful to AA and are always willing to co-operate with it in every way possible.

"Tradition Seven

Every group ought to be fully self-supporting, declining outside contributions.

"Why should a group refuse donation from some interested outsider? Most societies are very glad to receive such help.

"Early experience, here as with other Traditions, has been the teacher.

"In the first place, a group has very little need of money, just enough for rent, refreshments, lights, and contributions to national and local service centers, such as Al-Anon's Headquarters, and the local intergroup association or council.[111] Any considerable amount above these requirements might be a temptation to enter other fields, thus inviting unnecessary argument and dissension.

"In the next place, if Headquarters were to receive large outside donations, the whole fabric of Al-Anon's interrelationship would be changed. Headquarters, not needing the groups' support, might be tempted to act in an authoritative way instead of serving the groups and reflecting their experience as it does now. The groups themselves, thinking Headquarters had enough money, might no longer feel responsible to it and might drift away on their own.

"Furthermore, strings often are attached to large outside donations. It is only too true that 'purse strings frequently lead to other strings which sometimes turn into ropes.' Al-Anon might become bound to an outside policy and so lose its freedom.

"An instance of how an outside gift of money or its equivalent results in pressure of one kind or another follows:

"A group secured a meeting place in a church building. They offered to pay a small rental for the use of the room, but the minister said he was glad to let such a worthy society use it free of charge. But at every single meeting the minister gave a long religious talk. The group couldn't object because of his generosity in giving them the use of the room. Although some of the older members received much benefit from the sermons, new members were only confused by them and didn't come back a second time. The purpose of the group was being lost. Finally they had to move to quarters where they paid rent.

"For the fellowship it has become clear that the simpler way is best: accept no outside contributions large or small.

---

111. This refers to Al-Anon information services (AISs).

"Tradition Eight

Al-Anon Twelfth Step work should remain forever non-professional, but our service centers may employ special workers.

"There are many paid workers in the fields of welfare, religion, and medicine who can be of much service to the families of alcoholics. But there is a special place for help given by one who has experienced the same suffering and who knows from the inside what the other's feelings and problems must be. This identification, as we call it in AA and Al-Anon, brings a warm glow of reassurance to the newcomer. She knows she is no longer alone with her problem, that she is understood. There is nothing quite like the camaraderie so engendered.

"What if this were paid for? Much of its spontaneity, much of its mutuality, and most of its value to the helper would be lost. Truly, in giving we receive. The helper, perhaps herself a newcomer who is depressed and low because of her failure to aid her alcoholic husband, received a great lift when she recognized that here is a field where her own hard experience can be uniquely useful. With deep satisfaction and gratitude, she tells the newer one just how she herself has been helped, how her own changed attitudes have relieved her tensions, how she has begun to hope.

"A new member is sometimes so grateful for what she has received in Al-Anon that she wants to give her sponsor a lovely gift. The sponsor, without being ungracious, can explain to the newcomer that obligation in Al-Anon reaches forward, not backward; that she could best pay for her own improved outlook by helping newer members to improve theirs.

Thus this non-professional Twelfth Step is the ladder up which members help each other to climb into the light.

"But our Al-Anon service centers, which spread the knowledge of our program throughout the area, country or world do need regular office personnel. Experience has shown us that these workers should be paid at as near the going rate as possible for the positions they hold, even though they may be Al-Anon members. A member's personal knowledge of Al-Anon is of great value in such an office, but she is paid for her office work only.

"Tradition Nine

Our groups, as such, ought never be organized; but we may create service centers or committees directly responsible to those they serve.

"When newcomers are told that Al-Anon has no organization, no president with authority to govern, no treasurer who can compel payment of dues, and no board of directors who can oust members— when they learn that no Al-Anon member is in a position to give another a directive or to enforce obedience—they are astounded.

"We are fortunate in not needing much organization. Too much personal authority tends to stifle an enthusiastic response to Al-Anon's principles.

"It was from experiences such as the following that we learned the wisdom of this Tradition.

"A member of one of the early Al-Anon centers moved to a new town where she started an Al-Anon group. Because there was no literature as yet and no other group in the area, this member set herself up as the sole authority on Al-Anon. She told her group just what they should do, how they should do it, and who should belong. The group, grateful for her help and not knowing anything about the Al-Anon Traditions, suggested that no group be organized on a basis of personal authority. The "president," feeling the group owed her loyalty for all she had done for them, refused to resign. So the group simply re-formed itself without her.

"A group is usually set up with a chairman who conducts the meeting, a secretary who keeps the others informed on current Al-Anon events, and a treasurer who attends to the voluntary contributions.[112]

---

112. The 1966 revision added, in part: "...and a group representative who carries the wishes and ideas of the group to the area assembly and brings back to the group information which the delegate has obtained from the annual World Service Conference."

These positions give some form and shape to the meetings, and since a rotating system is invariably employed, no one person stays long in any position, and all have a chance to take responsibility.

"Our service centers or committees have a minimum of internal organization. But they must have enough to operate effectively. Headquarters and a few centers are incorporated in order to carry on their business more efficiently. They have no authority over the groups and they function as trusted servants, answering inquiries, helping groups with their problems, handling over-all public relations, and publishing literature.

"But as a spiritual entity, Al-Anon has no organization whatever.

"Tradition Ten

The Al-Anon Family Groups have no opinion on outside issues; hence our name ought never be drawn into public controversy.

"This Tradition is another precautionary principle to preserve Al-Anon's unity. It goes further than Tradition Six in its warnings. It suggests that Al-Anon, as such, ought not express opinions on the issues of the day, such as segregation, temperance, or any other public question.

"Our thousands of members are people of differing race and color, with different creeds, politics, and viewpoints. If we were to take sides on any of these public issues, we would surely be divided within. Our Al-Anon Family Groups' name and a free, unbiased, uncontroversial atmosphere in which to develop, belong to all.

"Though an Al-Anon group were to take up the cudgel for the improvement of such a universally regretted situation as juvenile delinquency, this might also divide us. Another group might disagree with the first group's ideas on how this condition could be remedied. Even if the resulting controversy did not reach the public level, it would separate and divert us.

"Fortunately, within the Traditions, Al-Anon is able to take a part in the alleviation of juvenile delinquency through the Alateen groups. This fact clearly points up the well-known truth that the best and surest way to improve the moral tone of a bad situation, public or personal, is by example. Each member of Al-Anon, in trying to live by Al-Anon's Twelve Steps, is doing a small but positive part toward raising the level of all.

"Tradition Eleven

Our public relations policy is based on attraction rather than promotion; we need always maintain personal anonymity at the level of press, radio, TV and films. We need guard with special care the anonymity of all AA members.

"Without their many outside well-wishers, neither AA nor Al-Anon could have grown as fast nor spread as they have. Good publicity has been a means of bringing members into both fellowships.

"Al-Anon is grateful when newspapers, magazines, TV, or films want to publicize our work. The only stipulations we make are that the presentation be accurate and that full names not be used.

"The public good will that AA and now Al-Anon enjoy resulted not only because of approval of much-needed good works but because of two very wise publicity policies which AA early instituted: attraction rather than promotion, and personal anonymity.

"Al-Anon inherited the benefits of the public's good opinion of AA, which AA earned the hard and sometimes the sensational way, as when an early promotion-minded alcoholic ballyhooed AA and himself on the radio, then got drunk.

"Attraction and promotion are differing approaches to the same end, public information. The difference between them is a matter not only of degree but of kind. 'Attraction' implies the quality of humility. This is well exemplified by Al-Anon anonymity at the public level, which means that we place principles before personalities. On the other hand 'promotion' often connotes certain high pressure methods of aggressive selling and self-interested persuasion.

"In addition to the anonymity at the public level of press, radio, films and TV which Al-Anon suggests, anonymity as a personal family matter should be considered. Since the policy of anonymity arose originally to protect new AA's from the stigma of alcoholism, it is up to the Al-Anon member to respect the alcoholic mate's choice in the matter. Where he wishes to draw the line among family, friends, church, community, there is where she, too, should draw it. Personal situations and the alcoholic's length of sobriety in AA may change this line from time to time.

"The Al-Anon member whose alcoholic is still drinking, or is dry but not in AA, should protect his anonymity with special care, because the former is even more sensitive than a sober alcoholic and the latter has not the satisfactions of membership in AA. And the recital in meetings of the alcoholic's escapades or his personal treatment of his wife should be avoided.

"Tradition Twelve

Anonymity is the spiritual foundation of all our Traditions, ever reminding us to place principles above personalities.

"Fortunately it was recognized early that the experiences of Alcoholics Anonymous as set down in the Steps and Traditions were spiritual principles which Al-Anon could use equally well.

"But long before that, when there were less than a hundred alcoholics in AA, over-eager enthusiasts shouted glad tidings of one another's recovery, telling too much too publicly. The result often was a violation of the newcomer's privacy.

"So the principle of anonymity was first instituted as a protection for the new AA member. Then, by degrees, its spiritual substance was recognized. Principles became more important than personalities.

"Now, although Al-Anon members may at first practice anonymity for the protection of their partners, they soon find that anonymity is real humility at work. It is the spirit of sacrifice, the willingness to give up personal desires for the sake of the group, the helping of others without pay or personal glory. It is an all-pervading spiritual quality which keynotes AA and Al-Anon everywhere.

"In this Tradition all the others are contained. Each of us takes part in weaving the protective mantle of anonymity which covers our whole society and under which we may grow and work in unity."

9. 1960 Revised Chapter, Al-Anon and the Family

This new text consolidated portions of the original chapters titled "The Family Group Program at Work," "The Sex Problem," and "Do Husbands of Alcoholics Need Family Groups, Too?" New subheadings were: "Social Contacts," "The Sex Problem," "Al-Anon for Men," and "Children of Alcoholics."

"Anyone living with an alcoholic knows how hard it is to create and maintain any sort of family life. There is a dangerous tendency, however, to blame these family problems entirely on the compulsive drinker. Alcoholism certainly contributes to divorce, juvenile delinquency, and mental illness but these conditions exist in countless homes where there is no drinking problem. Therefore we propose to take a look at family life in general before going on to Al-Anon's role in trying to help some of the situations that may be laid fairly at that door of alcoholism.

"Dr. Ruth Fox, Medical Director of the National Council on Alcoholism, reminds us that:

'The family was originally formed for security and procreation. Today, love and companionship are strong additional motives for marriage. As of old, the family should provide food, shelter and material necessities for its members, and, as of old, it should buttress against anxieties and establish the personal identity of each member as part of a loving, reassuring unit. Other functions of the family include the training of children for their various roles: work, sex, and social and creative development. Fulfillment of sex needs between husband and wife aids in solving conflicts and in building satisfactory self-images as mates who are happy in the performance of their privileges and duties.

'In a well-adjusted family the normal goals of security, pleasure, and self-expression should be attained without too much conflict. Tolerance of differences, respect for individuality, and a sharing of responsibility and authority make for healthy family life.

'Unfortunately, some of the stresses of modern living make this ideal picture difficult of attainment. The struggle of business competition has changed the role of the father to a large extent. He may no longer have time or energy to be the daily head of the household as he was a generation or so ago. His fear of economic insecurity may have undermined his old confidence. He may be afraid of other men in business and may carry over this anxiety to his home life. Father in many homes may indeed have become the 'forgotten man'; mother may have become the ruler of the household. She *seems* strong, self-reliant and aggressive. Actually, disappointed that she can no longer lean on her husband for authority and shared responsibility in the training of the children and management of the home, she is often confused and frightened. Unwillingly, she may be losing her femininity just as her husband may be losing his masculinity.

'The children suffer under this shift of roles. They often feel unable to look to their fathers for strength and guidance, and to their mothers for love and understanding. When this displacement of roles causes friction between the parents, the children are caught in family arguments and tension. They feel the need for escape, and they do it in loneliness or turn away from home entirely to seek companionship in unsupervised and often devious ways.

'If the family becomes too disturbed, it tends to become socially isolated, with the added unhappy result that its members are thrown into too close interaction. Often the mother who is alienated from the husband develops an unhealthy, smothering love for one or more of the children. Then instead of a warm, interdependent group, the family pairs off into warring factions: the men, big and little, line up against the women, or father and daughter close ranks against mother and son.'

"Let us remember that any and all of these deviations from a happy home life can happen to any family. And now may we consider how alcoholism adds to the trouble, and how Al-Anon is often able to ease some of these tensions.

"In families which have alcoholism to cope with, deviations from the ideal are the rule rather than the exception. Without her husband's help, the mother not only assumes the full burden of bringing up the children but also finds herself facing creditors, making up the deficiencies in the family income, and deciding all major issues.

"The assumption of her husband's duties creates both resentment and confusion in her. She is overworked, physically tired, nervously exhausted, and in fear for her sanity.

"In the household there is also resentment. He feels that his wife has undermined his manhood and has stolen his authority. The children, of course, are also affected by this shift in parental roles. They no longer have a father whom they can fully respect, nor a mother whom they can unreservedly love.

"When a boy loses his admiration for his father he may turn from the normal goals of manhood and develop an abnormal dependency on the mother. Conversely, when a daughter sees her father degraded, she often turns against her mother, whom she blames for her father's downfall.

"The social isolation that occurs in any disturbed family is heightened where alcoholism is the chief trouble because of the violence and family fights that take place. Truancy and juvenile delinquency often have their beginnings in such situations.

Social Contacts

"Social contacts outside the alcoholic's family present great difficulties, sometimes even greater than those within the family circle. Societies have taboos and frown on even small infractions, and our own society is no exception. A gross flouting of convention is cause for ostracism. The wife married to a man who constantly breaks the rules finds herself trying to walk a tightrope in a high wind: she loves this husband who behaves in such an alien way, and loyalty demands that she defend him against critics. Yet the people who criticize most are inevitably those who are closest—her parents, his parents, their closest friends, their children, and his employer. These are also the people whom she needs most and wants most to keep close to her, for only those deeply interested will take the trouble to speak openly. Others simply pull back from a situation what will embarrass them.

"The more she withdraws the more frustrated and lonely she becomes. It is here that Al-Anon can be helpful. Talking with others who have been through the same problem brings relief and hope to the bewildered non-alcoholic.

"She comes to realize that she did not cause her husband's alcoholism and cannot be expected to cure it. She sees that she not only can but should get back into the world. From the small, sympathetic group of Al-Anon she can move out into society where she will probably find that much of the criticism she endured will not be forthcoming now.

"Sometimes a husband will object violently to his wife's getting out into the world again. If so she must give the whole problem deep thought and probably consult her clergyman, her doctor, or a member of AA who, because of his own past, may be able to advise her. But it is generally agreed among those who have studied the question that the non-alcoholic is helped by becoming active again. It usually follows that when a wife is in a healthier frame of mind, her alcoholic also benefits.

"There is much she can do, and the more nearly normal her life is, the better for the whole family. Half a loaf is indeed better than no loaf at all. Some wives are able to become so free in their minds that they can invite guests to their homes, even when the possibility still exists of the husbands "making scenes." If this is not feasible, other activities are possible, especially if there are children or young people to be considered. Striving for normality may be difficult, but giving in to despair is even more painful, besides being quite useless.

"Then, in the happy event that the husband should decide to seek help for himself, the wife will be well on her way to a wholesome outlook, with many difficult adjustments already made.

The Sex Problem

"Sex is one of the most seriously affected areas in the home of an alcoholic. When the very basis of the love relationship changes it is not easy for a wife (or husband) to remember that alcoholism is a disease to be treated with understanding and tolerance. Often when a new member comes to Al-Anon for comfort and help, she wants desperately to know the answer to the tangled web of her sex life. Shyness and loyalty often keep her from voicing her insecurity. When the alcoholic is the wife, her husband may find it impossible to feel tenderness toward a maudlin and repulsive woman.

"Al-Anon groups are not authorities on marital relations. All that Al-Anon members can offer a troubled newcomer is the assurance that they too have suffered in this vital phase of their lives, and that some of them have found partial or complete solutions to their individual cases.

"Some women prefer to talk about such personal matters privately with an older member, whose suggestions will be offered as individual opinion rather than as authoritative advice.

"Whether or not the whole question of sex comes up for discussion in any particular Al-Anon group depends upon the wishes, viewpoint, and maturity of the members. As in other aspects of family affairs, good taste and concern for the dignity of the alcoholic as a human being should always prevent recital of too intimate details or complaints.

"However, realistic and objective approach to the sex problem can prove genuinely helpful both to Al-Anon members and to the alcoholic. In Al-Anon there is an opportunity to bring out into the open the fears and resentments that have been festering and to show that they are typical of alcoholism rather than personal and isolated burdens. Members should not attempt to give specific advice but they can clarify thinking, tell their own solutions if they care to and suggest sources of professional help when it is needed.

"Such discussion can do much to make a harried wife aware of the changes in the sex relationship that are typical of an alcoholic. It is important that she understand that her husband's increased or decreased sexual demands are symptoms that have little bearing on his love for her; that uninhibited behavior, lack of tenderness, or even lack of cleanliness, are not uncommon phases of alcoholism that affect her reaction to her husband when he is drunk and frequently set up an aversion to him when he is sober. These discussions sometimes reveal to a wife that she has been rejecting her husband unkindly and unjustifiably to suit her preferences, and that she needs to extend a more loving understanding of his difficulties in this area of their lives.

"It may be at least cold comfort to realize that an alcoholic's promiscuous behavior toward other women does not necessarily mean he does not love his wife. What to do when such actions lead to sordid and serious results is usually a matter for medical or legal advice and not within the scope of one woman's opinion to another. But Al-Anon members can be a source of great comfort during these periods of stress. Often their understanding makes it possible for the unhappy wife to withhold drastic action, and even bitterness, as testified by the evidently low divorce rate among well-established AA and Al-Anon couples.

"When a member is faced with a serious and persistent sex problem that threatens her marriage it is usually indicated that she should seek professional advice. Wisdom suggests that she get help before rancors grow too deep for healing. Wives, particularly young ones, sometimes complain that their husband's "outrageous behavior" when drunk has married their unity permanently. This hopeless attitude is never more regrettable than when the husband has joined AA and is making an earnest effort to stop drinking and regain the respect and affection of his wife. Competent counsel may tide over the crisis and do much to help both partners to renew the marriage. Many an alcoholic has noticed a happy change in his wife after he has had an opportunity in Al-Anon to learn a more understanding attitude toward her partner.

Al-Anon for Men

"While there are some differences between the situation facing a man married to an alcoholic and a woman married to one, the problem is essentially the same.

"A man may go to Al-Anon while his wife is still drinking, but just as often he goes after she is well-established in AA. He may shrink from attending a group, feeling that he should not be called upon to give any additional time to his wife's recovery now that she has found the answers to her problem. But this is where some of the trouble lies: he considers it *her* problem, not his.

"He may envisage an Al-Anon meeting as a sort of ladies' Kaffeeklatsch and may want none of it. But he may go anyhow in order to indulge his wife and make her feel he is interested in the effort and progress she is making. He will probably find a few other men there. Moreover he will realize that it is from the whole group, not just men, that he will get understanding. He will find people who have been through what he has been through, people who have risen above ill-luck or ill-treatment and have learned to live normal lives.

"There have been times when the men in an Al-Anon group have considered breaking off to form a stag group, not because they feel uncomfortable in the co-educational atmosphere but because they think other men might come more willingly to an all-male group. There is at least one such group on the West Coast and another is starting in New York City. But most groups decide against such separation. The same situation in reverse was true in AA in its early days when it was made up almost entirely of men. The occasional woman who came felt out of place and reluctant to 'take her hair down.'

"While most of the problems of men and women in Al-Anon are alike, there are a few areas which present different and specific difficulties. For example:

Economics: It is well-known that fewer husbands stick with an alcoholic than do wives, and one of the reasons is because of the economic situation. In most families the husband is the bread-winner. He may lose jobs and spend on liquor what should have gone to his family; nevertheless, more often than not, he does support the family. Because he is self-supporting he can leave his wife, whereas the wife of an alcoholic very often stays with him because she can't support herself and the children.

"When the wife is the alcoholic, the economic problem is different. The harried husband is faced with having his income wasted by someone who seems to have no respect for his efforts, his ability, or his feelings. She takes no interest in the home, and be becomes ashamed of it. The money he gives her to pay the bills, for instance, or to buy food, is spent on liquor. The electricity gets turned off, the refrigerator and the pantry are empty, and the same old threadbare chair stands in the living room. And there is often added threat that his woman is hurting his career, his standing with the boss, his clients or customers.

"*Social*: Both the husband of an alcoholic and a wife of an alcoholic are faced with the same reluctance to bring friends and acquaintances home for dinner. But the husband has one advantage, he can take them out. He has the usual problem about going to other people's houses, especially the classic problem of leaving a party early under the alcoholic's loud protests. The host is made uncomfortable, and little by little, people stop inviting them. This pattern, well-known to the woman with an alcoholic husband, has added to it a certain shame of the man who realizes that other men look down on a husband who cannot control his wife. He senses that he is regarded as weak and unmanly. The advice he gets from other men is not, "Why don't you leave her?" but often, "What she needs is to learn who's boss."

"*Children*: It is no easier for a man than for a woman to assume the roles of both parents. In some ways it is more difficult. A woman who is home for most of the day is at least on hand to do her part as a mother. When the woman is an alcoholic, the whole burden rests on the father, and there is the added problem of having had a drunken mother around the house all day. The short time he can spend at home is never enough to do the necessary chores: buying food, collecting soiled clothes and taking them to the laundry, finding someone to come in and do the cleaning. Often we must try to do something about the children, whom he may find huddles in a closed room, too frightened to come out. They may be sick with colds or upset stomachs, and no one has taken care of them or called the doctor.

"As the children grow older they may become resentful. They not only refuse to bring friends home but often stay away themselves, making it necessary for the father to embark on a telephone search or to go out looking for them.

"Even after he has brought order out of the chaos he finds awaiting him, he has the discouraging conviction that it will all have to be done over again the next day or so.

"*Sex:* Every drunk is repulsive. Everyone married to a drunk knows that, and sooner or later must face the problem. Sometimes the wife suffers physical violence when she withdraws from the amorous advances of a drunken husband. When the wife is the alcoholic and finds her husband lacking in interest, she reacts in *her* way. Perhaps she weeps violently and accuses him of no longer caring for her, thus giving her cause to drink. Sometimes he gets away and seeks the companionship of another woman. Or he may be unable to feel affection or emotion for any woman, associating the entire sex with the distaste he feels for his wife. If the husband tends to drink less and less, not because he feels 'holier' than his wife but because he is disenchanted with the whole business of liquor, his wife almost always looks upon his abstinence as a silent but vehement criticism.

"Once a wife joins AA and stops drinking, both she and her husband have to make the slow journey back to normality. Going to Al-Anon can show the husband how seriously he, the non-alcoholic, has changed through the years of tension and strain.

"The Twelve Steps of AA become part of the lives of both husband and wife, if they will work at them. Al-Anons have 'slips' in much the same way that alcoholics do. There come times when the non-alcoholic feels that he no longer needs Al-Anon, or he feels that he should get out of the rut he is in and have a taste of the world that never needs to cope with the ogre of alcoholism. Whatever causes the slip is not important. The only thing that is important is that a non-alcoholic husband needs Al-Anon, not occasionally but all the time. One man put it this way:

'It has become and must remain an integral part of my life, the frame around the picture that is me. Without it my edges begin to curl, my fabric to warp, my paint begins to crack.'

"Once in Al-Anon, the non-alcoholic husband like his feminine counterpart, learns to live in the light of certain insights:

"First, that his wife is suffering from a progressive incurable disease.

"Second, that while there is nothing he can do to cure her or to prevent her from drinking, he can help her immeasurably by reaching out to her in love and understanding.

"Third, recognizing that he is powerless over his wife's alcoholic problem, that he must learn to live his own life as best he can in any event.

"Fourth, that except for his wife's problem with booze he shares every other aspect of life with her, that in Al-Anon he can learn to accept this fact, to face these problems, and to seek answers.

"Fifth, that many problems are not capable of solution without help, and that while some help comes from sharing experiences, the greatest help can come only from a Higher Power; one must learn to surrender one's great problems to this Higher Power, accepting the fact that the difficulties of life will always be with us, but that God will never burden us with more than we can bear.

Children of Alcoholics

"A home with an alcoholic parent is a dreary if not tragic setting for children. They are constantly immersed in confusion, and they grope for guidance, for love, and for peace. Unhappy within their own home, they are often just as miserable outside it, exposed to taunts from schoolmates and unwelcome pity from grownups. Fear, lack of sleep and food, and lack of normal family fun combine to make children withdrawn or openly hostile.

"As the non-alcoholic parent in Al-Anon begins to learn more and more about alcoholism as an illness, she becomes more objective. The children find her more consistent, and the guilt and anxiety which they had previously felt diminishes. They gradually understand that the drinking is compulsive and not caused by either their own or their mother's behavior. Hope is renewed for these youngsters when they discover that alcoholism is a disease. Many of them are helped to a better understanding of the problem by joining Alateen groups."

10. Al-Anon Is for Women

The following text was added to the chapter "Al-Anon and the Family" in 1974 and the sub-heading was added in September 1976.

"Families with alcoholism to cope with, however, find such problems the rule rather than the exception. Deprived of her husband's help by his excessive drinking, the mother must make decisions for the family, assume responsibility for rearing the children, face creditors and perhaps even work outside the home to make up deficiencies in the family income.

"The necessity to take over her husband's duties creates resentment and confusion in her. She is overworked, nervously exhausted and perhaps always doubtful of her ability to carry all this responsibility.

"The husband, notwithstanding his inability to cope with the problems which have fallen on his wife's shoulders, may resent, however unjustly, that his wife has assumed his male prerogatives, usurped his authority. The children are affected by these shifts in parental roles. They no longer have a father whom they can fully respect nor a mother whom they can unreservedly love. When a boy loses his respect for his father he may turn away from the normal masculine goals and develop dependency and perhaps identification with the mother. When the daughter sees her father in a degraded condition, she may actually sympathize with him and blame her mother for her father's drinking.

"The social isolation that occurs in any disturbed family is increased when alcoholism is the chief problem."

11. 1958 Revision Regarding Alateen Groups

Lois asked for the following paragraphs to be in the 1958 revision:

"Since this book was first published a thrilling new companion fellowship has evolved, called Alateens. This society was started in 1956[113] in Pasadena, California, by young people, who, having gone to AA and Al-Anon with their parents, realized that neither meetings quite fulfilled their own needs. Even at Al-Anon special youth meetings, they did not feel free to discuss many of their problems. Therefore they decided to hold their own meetings where they could more effectively help themselves and others with a like problem.

"Their idea has spread extensively and many new groups are being formed....They follow the Twelve Steps and Twelve Traditions and use the AA slogans and Serenity Prayer. Any young person with an alcoholic problem in the family[114], whether his relative is in AA or not, is welcome in the group.

---

113. This "society" officially became Alateen in September 1957.

114. or in a friend

"It can well be imagined what unity of purpose this new fellow-ship can bring to the families of AA and Al-Anon, and what ben-eficial effect it can have, not only on the many problems of juve-niles of today, but on the well-being of the citizens of tomorrow."

12. Alateen Groups[115]

"Alateen sprang up to fill a family need, in very much the same way that Al-Anon was born. For many years the adolescent children of alcoholics received much help from their parents' and their own attendance at AA and Al-Anon meetings. Some of them learned long before they reached their teens that the alcoholic in the fami-ly was a sick person and not a weak-willed or intentionally unkind parent. Many of them grew up to admire the change that AA and Al-Anon made in their parents and were grateful for the improve-ment in their daily lives. In some cases informed teen-agers actually have been responsible for guiding their alcoholic parents to AA.

"Just as the relatives of alcoholics, however, found they needed association with others who understood their particular problem, so did a high-school boy in California back in 1957 feel the urge to talk to other teen-agers about his own adjustment to a troubled alcoholic family life. His story is almost as wonderful as that of the co-founders of AA.

"Bob was the son of an alcoholic father. He got in such serious trouble that he seemed destined for enrollment in a special school for problem children. His mother, active in Al-Anon, persuaded the school officials to give Bob one more chance. She and her hus-band begged the lad to try applying the Twelve Steps to his daily life. He began going with his parents to AA meetings and to Al-Anon with his mother. The meetings helped Bob, but he still felt frustrated; these grownup problems weren't *his* problems. And so he hit upon the idea of forming a group of teen-age children of Alcoholics Anonymous, and this was the beginning of Alateen.

---

115. This chapter was added to the text in 1960.

"Bob was right in believing that teen-agers would welcome a group of their own. Al-Anon and AA members helped this first group of adolescents live through its birth pangs. In less than a year the group grew from five to twenty-three active members. It set the pattern and established procedures that have been followed basically ever since. Today the movement is growing steadily.[116]

"The age range of Alateen groups at first covered the literal thirteen to nineteen bracket; today some groups stretch the limits to include twelve to twenty year olds. Some Alateen groups split in half so that the younger members meet separately from the older teenagers.

"It is customary for an Alateen group to have an advisor from AA or Al-Anon,[117] who may start the meeting or be a silent guest joining in the discussion only on request. Some groups hold meetings with no adult present.[118] Most teenagers prefer an advisor who is not the parent of anyone in the group.

"Meetings are held in homes of members or in another room of the same public building that houses AA or Al-Anon groups, and at the same time.

"Alateen, like Al-Anon, is separate from AA, and forms a vital link in the family program of looking squarely at alcoholism and trying to do something about living with it in greater sanity and happiness. Like AA and Al-Anon, Alateen members attempt to live by the Twelve Steps and their adapted version of the Twelve Traditions.[119] The Serenity Prayer plays an important role in their lives.

"Most Alateen groups are self-supporting through collections or small monthly contributions, but a few Al-Anon or AA groups

---

116. Alateen registered groups as of the year 2000 total 2,700.

117. Today these advisors are known as Alateen sponsors and are Al-Anon members. AA members do not sponsor an Alateen group but can assist an Alateen sponsor who is an Al-Anon member.

118. See Policy Digest, Membership and Group Meetings/Conventions, Alateen Groups section in the *Al-Anon/Alateen Service Manual*.

119. Alateen's Twelve Traditions were adapted from Al-Anon's in 1957 and sent to the existing Alateen groups for approval.

assume expenses of Alateens until the group has grown enough to pay its own way.[120]

"There is something inspiring and reassuring about the way in which Alateen meets the needs of children in alcoholic homes. Trying to live by the same Twelve Steps that guide their parents gives them a sense of family solidarity. Going with one or both parents to a meeting builds a sense of security that far surpasses the old pattern of being left alone at home. Beginning to have faith in a Higher Power, perhaps for the first time in years or in their lives, does a great deal to restore peace to an adolescent who may have been too embarrassed by an alcoholic parent to go to church or Sunday school.

"Alateens take the responsibility of holding office very seriously. Officers are elected and function just as in Al-Anon. A teen-ager who may be a frightened and seemingly unimportant member of the family can often gain self-confidence as the chairman of the group, responsible for opening the meeting with a moment of silence or prayer. Reading the Twelve Steps and Twelve Traditions, as many groups do, gives an adolescent new dignity.

"As the members of the group plan meetings together, they draw comfort and interest from each other. Inviting guest speakers—AA or Al-Anon members, a school official, a judge, a doctor, etc.— opens up new contacts and new ideas, and often leads to consultation with the group advisor.[121] Being part of a group that is very definitely their own fills a lonely void.

"Alateen meetings provide pleasure along with information and hope. Fun and talk and refreshments follow the serious program.

"Alateens honor AA and Al-Anon anonymity, and are even more insistent than grownups in placing principles above personalities.

---

120. See Policy Digest, Finances, Fund-Raising section in the *Al-Anon/Alateen Service Manual*.

121. The group advisor is now known as a group sponsor. See Al-Anon & Alateen Groups at Work, Meeting Ideas, Outside Speakers section in the *Al-Anon/Alateen Service Manual*.

13. Al-Anon and the Community[122]

"For many years AA has played a vital part in the community understanding and control of alcoholism. Al-Anon is assuming a similar role in widening public awareness of alcoholism as a family disease and in putting families in touch with the social forces that are equipped to help them.

"Al-Anon is a non-professional fellowship, but individual members may recommend understanding doctors or clergymen or lawyers to troubled relatives of alcoholics, and may direct members to sources which can give impartial and expert advice.

Social Agencies

"Although some of us have not been affected financially by an irresponsible problem drinker, there are many more to whom illness, non-support, unemployment, desertion, and imprisonment are familiar complications. To these people, words of comfort are not enough.

"Those who require counseling and referral services can obtain them at the National Council on Alcoholism[123] which has established local committees in many of the larger cities in the United States.

"Information on non-profit resources for employment, child guidance, and vocational training in occupational fields can all be obtained from various agencies in most cities.

"For those non-alcoholic partners who find it necessary to work themselves but have small children, there are Day-care, Homemakers' Service or Temporary Placement agencies almost everywhere.

Medical and Psychiatric Help

"The medical profession and AA have cooperated for so long in most communities that local AAs are usually well aware of the doc-

---

122. This chapter was added to the text in 1960.

123. The National Council on Alcoholism is now known as the National Council on Alcoholism and Drug Dependency (NCADD).

tors in town who treat alcoholism. In some places AA has a special relationship with a hospital that accepts alcoholics as patients.

"Many busy medical men have not the time to treat alcoholics because they lie about their drinking, refuse to follow directions, show up drunk for appointments, and do not really want to stop drinking. In short, alcoholics make time-consuming and unresponsive patients. There are, however, an increasing number of doctors who have both the information and the understanding so vitally necessary in these situations.

"A reliable source of help in finding the kind of medical care which an alcoholic needs is the National Council on Alcoholism through its nearest local committee. They will give you lists of doctors and psychiatrists; they will also provide lists of rest homes, shelters, clinics, and hospitals that treat alcoholism. In many localities today there are Alcoholism Information Centers and official agencies such as alcoholic rehabilitation programs, often sponsored by the Department of Health.

"It is possible that you or some other member of the family may need professional help in addition to the therapy[124] which Al-Anon affords. If so, the above sources give you the best chance of finding a doctor or psychiatrist who will be able to meet your particular needs.

Clerical Counsel

"In dealing with the problem of alcoholism in your home, your own minister, priest, or rabbi may be a great comfort to you and the rest of the family, because many clergymen have accepted the concept of alcoholism as a disease. More and more clergymen are taking a deep and sympathetic interest in the problem of the alcoholic, and counselors of this kind are to be greatly prized.

---

124. Today we use the term "mutual support."

"In this area, too, AA and Al-Anon members may be able to guide you to clergymen of your particular faith who are informed and who approach the alcoholic and you with understanding.

Legal Aid

"Families of alcoholics sometimes become involved involuntarily with the law or must turn to it for help. There are a lucky few who live in cities where police officers have been trained to consult the alcoholic's doctor, his family, and his employer before any court action is taken. This sort of community action is growing but is still rare.

"Specific information about legal aid is available from local welfare agencies. An increasing number of domestic relations courts throughout the country have staff psychiatrists who are competent to give help in alcoholic situations. Mental hygiene clinics, probation departments, and the courts themselves are often helpful to the alcoholic and his family.

Employers' Cooperation

"One of the most hopeful aspects of awareness of alcoholism as a disease lies in industry's fairly recent attitude. It is now common knowledge that progressive organizations such as Du Pont, Eastman Kodak, Consolidated Edison, to mention only a few, have well-conceived and executed rehabilitation programs for alcoholics in their employ. Thus the alcoholic wage earner stands a good chance in many companies of being helped instead of fired. Someone from the firm, an immediate supervisor or a fellow worker, directs the alcoholic to the Medical Department,[125] which in turn puts him in touch with AA, often with another employee who is a member. The wife who has tried to conceal her husband's drinking from his boss is surprised and relieved when someone in the organization enlists her help in carrying out the program for the alcoholic.

---

125. Medical departments are now known as Employee Assistance Programs (EAP)

"In a company without such facilities, there is greater danger of loss of job. Since wives often make the least successful bridges to AA, it is helpful if the employer or a co-worker uses his influence on the alcoholic. This recognition of the problem by the employer may be the spur to action that the alcoholic needed. In any event, co-operation between an alcoholic and his employer has a far greater chance of successful outcome than it did before industry took an enlightened interest in the problem."

14. Revision of Introduction to "They Found Answers"[126]

"Personal stories are sometimes more helpful than any other explanation of Al-Anon. Perhaps you will find in the following pages a story similar to your own. Varieties of experience are included: stories about wives whose husbands are still drinking, stories about wives with sober partners in AA, about husbands who are working the program with their alcoholic wives, and about the trials and triumphs of parents and children of alcoholics."

15. Revision to "His Way, Not Mine"[127]

"The foregoing was written five years ago and little has changed except that the opening sentence should read, 'I have now lived with an alcoholic for more than 28[128] years.' It is possible to say this only because of Al-Anon. Without its teachings I would long since have given up the struggle and cried quits. But once having accepted the idea that alcoholism is a disease, I have never felt free to leave since I know in my heart that if Jim suffered from any other ailment, no matter how personally demanding, I'd have seen him through it without question. I cannot see that alcoholism is any excuse for me to leave him. I have no quarrel with others who feel differently but as in all Al-Anon, this is my own decision to make.

---

126. In the 1960 edition the following preface was added to the text of this section. Some stories were removed in total; others remained the same as the original edition, with some minor changes in later editions.

127. In the 1960 revision the following ending was added and the story was retitled "But for the Grace of Al-Anon".

128. Later 28 years was changed to 30.

"I hope and pray that some time Jim will really return to AA and live it honestly and wholeheartedly. I hope that day comes soon. But it is because of Al-Anon and those early days at Headquarters, that I have such hope."

16. Revision to "A Father Works it Out"[129]

"Nearly twenty years have passed since Bob was restored to his family through AA — twenty years during which we have been richly repaid for whatever trouble we had while Bob was drinking.

"Sobriety always brings in its wake a flow of blessings beyond reckoning, and these were very real for us. I look upon them as something in the nature of a loan on which God expects payments to be made in service.

"Al-Anon offers the opportunity for such service in trying to carry the message to others, and for this I am sincerely grateful."

17. Revised Suggested Welcome[130]

"We welcome you to the _____ Al-Anon Family Group and hope you will find in this fellowship the help and friendship we have been privileged to enjoy.

"We who live[131] with the problem of alcoholism understand as perhaps few others can. We, too, were lonely and frustrated, but in Al-Anon we discover that no situation is really hopeless, and that it is possible for us to find contentment, and even happiness, whether the alcoholic is still drinking or not.

"We urge you to try our program. It will show you how to[132] find solutions that lead to serenity. So much depends on our own attitudes, and as we learn to place our problem in its true perspective, we find it loses its power to dominate our thoughts and our lives.

---

129. The following three paragraphs replaced the last two paragraphs of the original text beginning with the 1960 printing.125. The words "or have lived" were added in 1981.

130. This version is from the May 1973, 4th printing.

131. The words "or have lived" were added in 1981.

132. This text was changed to "It has helped many of us" in 1982.

"The family situation is bound to improve as we apply the Al-Anon ideas. Without such spiritual help, living with an alcoholic is too much for most of us. Our thinking becomes distorted by trying to force solutions and we become irritable and unreasonable without knowing it.

"The Al-Anon program is based on the Twelve Suggested Steps of Alcoholics Anonymous[133] which we try, little by little, one day at a time, to apply to our lives, along with our slogans and the Serenity Prayer. The loving interchange of help among members and daily reading of Al-Anon literature thus make us ready to receive the priceless gift of serenity."

18a. Preamble To The Twelve Steps[134][135]

"The Al-Anon Family Groups are a fellowship of relatives and friends of alcoholics who share their experience, strength and hope in order to solve their common problem of living with an alcoholic, and to help others do the same. We believe alcoholism is an illness which can be arrested, and that changed family attitudes can often aid recovery.

"The only requirement for membership is that there be a relative or a friend with a drinking problem. There are no dues for membership. Al-Anon is self-supporting through its own voluntary contributions.

"Al-Anon is not allied with any sect, denomination, political entity, organization or institution; does not engage in any controversy; neither endorses nor opposes any cause. Our primary purpose is to practice the Al-Anon program so we may help others with similar problems, to aid the alcoholic through understanding, and to grow spiritually ourselves."

---

133. This text was changed to "...Twelve Steps (adapted from Alcoholics Anonymous)..." in 1982.

134. This is the version used from 1966 to 1971.

135. The following text was added in 1984: "Al-Anon is an anonymous fellowship. Everything that is said here, in the group meeting and member-to-member, must be held in confidence. Only in this way can we feel free to say what is in our minds and hearts, for this is how we help one another in Al-Anon."

18b. Preamble To The Twelve Steps

This is the version used from 1973 to present.

"The Al-Anon Family Groups are a fellowship of relatives and friends of alcoholics who share their experience, strength, and hope in order to solve their common problems. We believe alcoholism is a family illness and that changed attitudes can aid recovery.

"Al-Anon is not allied with any sect, denomination, political entity, organization, or institution; does not engage in any controversy; neither endorses nor opposes any cause. There are no dues for membership. Al-Anon is self-supporting through its own voluntary contributions.

"Al-Anon has but one purpose: to help families of alcoholics. We do this by practicing the Twelve Steps, by welcoming and giving comfort to families of alcoholics, and by giving understanding and encouragement to the alcoholic."

19. Suggested Closing

The Suggested Closing was added to the text with the fourth printing of the Revised Expanded Version in May 1973.

"In closing, I would like to say that the opinions expressed here were strictly those of the person who gave them. Take what you liked and leave the rest.

"The things you heard were spoken in confidence and should be treated as confidential. Keep them within the walls of this room and the confines of your mind.

"A few special words to those of you who haven't been with us long: Whatever your problems, there are those among us who have had them, too. If you try to keep an open mind, you will find help. You will come to realize that there is no situation too difficult to be bettered and no unhappiness too great to be lessened.

"We aren't perfect. The welcome we give you may not show the warmth we have in our hearts for you. After a while, you'll discover that though you may not like all of us, you'll love us in a very special way—the same way we already love you.

"Talk to each other, reason things out with someone else, but let there be no gossip or criticism of one another. Instead, let the understanding, love and peace of the program grow in you one day at a time.

"Will all who care to, join me in the closing prayer."[136]

20. (Al-Anon) Family Group Literature

All of part IV, "Family Group Literature," was deleted with the second printing and the following substituted:

"Besides this book, Al-Anon Headquarters publishes a monthly periodical, The Family Group Forum, and an annual World Directory of groups. Headquarters has various pamphlets on alcoholism, personal stories and reprints about Al-Anon from national magazines. There are leaflets about the Al-Anon purposes, about Headquarters, how to start a group, etc.

"At the International AA Convention at St. Louis in 1955 Al-Anon held four separate sessions and these talks by Family Group members from all parts of the country are available in four pamphlets: Lois' Talk; The Twelve Steps; Family Adjustments and The Children of Alcoholics.

A price list of all literature will be sent upon request.

━•━ ⚔ ━•━

"All AA literature can, of course, be purchased from AA General Service Headquarters (NY). *The AA Grapevine*, which

---

136. In 1995 the wording was changed to read, "Will all who care to, join me in closing with the _____ prayer?" See Al-Anon/Alateen Groups at Work, Meeting Format, Suggested Closing section, *Al-Anon/Alateen Service Manual.*

often includes stories about families of alcoholics, is published monthly by the Alcoholics Anonymous Grapevine, Inc. NY."

21. Adoption of Conference Approved Literature—1961 World Service Conference

"Reasons for the adoption of the Conference approval concept are outlined in the 1961 Conference Summary.

(p. 91) "Conference approval for literature was further redefined in the Summary the following year.... By 1965, the Conference was ready to stand firm on the Conference Approval concept. Alice B., by now Literature Chairman, explains why in a statement attached to the 1965 Conference Summary."

Alice's statement reads:

"Conference Approved Literature Mirrors The Al-Anon Image

"Al-Anon is coming of age. All around us are signs of our growing importance in the fight against alcoholism. The patient, unselfish work of Al-Anon members and volunteers is gaining recognition as a powerful force coping with this world-wide sickness.

"We have taken some giant strides in the past year. Al-Anon is being accepted as a source of real help by such professional organizations as the National Council on Alcoholism and its affiliates, (NCA)[137], and the North American Association of Alcoholism Programs, (NAAAP),[138] which includes all the publicly-supported alcoholism centers on this continent.

"The latter, for the first time in Al-Anon's history, invited us to sit in on a conference of its executives and directors, where we had the privilege of explaining Al-Anon's role in the work of helping the families of alcoholics, in order to develop better lines of communication between Al-Anon and NAAAP.

"This kind of recognition gives Al-Anon new stature and dignity. We are long past the phase when we appeared to the world as

---

137. The National Council on Alcoholism is now the National Council on Alcoholism and Drug Dependency, (NCADD).

138. This association no longer exists.

clusters of desperate housewives huddled together for comfort and simple answers to complex problems. We have taken our place among the professionals in the field of alcoholic work.

"But growing up also creates new problems against which we must assert our unity, and our determination not to be diverted from our primary purpose. That purpose is to help the families of alcoholics to live full and satisfying lives despite the difficulties they have to cope with.

"One of the major problems that confronts us in our coming-of-age is that a united fellowship like ours is a tempting target for people who want to profit from what we have built. Private publishers, for example, are offering their printed matter to many of our groups. There is no way of knowing how many there are, but the danger to our fellowship is present and active. Sometimes the leaflets and booklets they offer are good inspirational material, but this does not mean they represent Al-Anon ideas; sometimes they are poor, the grammar and spelling so questionable and the printing so slovenly, their use hurts not only the groups involved, but all of Al-Anon. And when the copy _is_ sound Al-Anon doctrine, it has often been pirated from our own literature.

"There is only one way to protect ourselves from the inroads made by these outsiders, and that is for our groups to refuse to use their Al-Anon funds for any but Conference Approved literature. As individuals, we are free to buy and read anything we want to, but as members of a fellowship in which we gratefully share a new way of life, we want to protect the Al-Anon image by following the guidance of our Twelve Traditions.

"The First Tradition says: 'Our common welfare should come first; personal progress for the greatest number depends on unity.'

"Living up to this Tradition means delivering the Al-Anon message without distortion or dilution, by using only the literature which has been carefully prepared and screened to reflect _Al-Anon as a whole._

"Our Second Tradition says: 'Our leaders are but trusted servants; they do not govern.' Among those who serve are the members of the Literature Committee, ten in number,[139], and the staff and volunteers at HQ. They are dedicated to the task of making our literature correct in approach and content, as well as in language used to express Al-Anon ideas. These servants are worthy of confidence.

"Our Fourth Tradition says: 'Each group should be autonomous, _except in matters affecting another group, or Al-Anon and AA as a whole._' It is true that we are autonomous, but that does not give us the right to use the Al-Anon name in ways that could affect the fellowship adversely. When one part of Al-Anon publishes literature which is not Conference-Approved, it is a serious threat to Al-Anon unity. There are even now thousands of pieces of literature being distributed in the name of Al-Anon which are marred by misspellings, grammatical errors, inappropriate material, distortions of Al-Anon principles and even gross corruption's of the Twelve Steps, which we are privileged to use through the generosity of AA.[140] We thus hurt not only our own fellowship, but AA, to whom we owe so much.

"This is not to say that _some_ of the literature is not excellent. It is! But if Group X prints a good piece of literature, Group Z is just as free to publish one that may hurt the Al-Anon image.

"Two years ago, the WSC, in the persons of our own elected delegates, voted to use only Conference-Approved literature. Our continued unity and growth depend upon our living up to this decision.

"The Literature Committee receives most gratefully, and often uses, ideas suggested by groups and intergroups. This is a vital part of the information that enables us to do the job for the benefit of all Al-Anon. Working as a central clearing house, we are able to maintain a balanced list of literature to meet the varied needs of our

---

139. The Literature Committees are now 36 in number.

140. In the early days of Al-Anon, groups published their own literature. Since 1961 all Al-Anon literature has followed the CAL process and is produced by the World Service Office as directed by the World Service Conference.

far-flung groups _and to get the most mileage our of every Al-Anon dollar spent_. Duplication would waste money that could be used to print much-needed new material for the whole fellowship.

"The members of the Literature Committee are well-fitted to write and edit Al-Anon literature. The quality of our booklets and leaflets is evidence of this, and all of them play an active and constructive role in every writing project. Every word is weighed and measured, not only for its pertinence to a particular problem, but in its relation to the other on our list.

"Our booklets are in demand by many of the public services in the field of alcoholism who use them in working with the families of alcoholics. A recent order for over $200 worth of Al-Anon literature was accompanied by this statement: 'This literature is being made available to our officers in order that they may interest their clients whom we meet in Juvenile and Family Court. We have found that Al-Anon has had better than average success in helping the partner or the child of an alcoholic.'

"We have the inestimable blessing of the counsel of Lois and a group of early volunteers. The total of their experience covers many years of struggle with Al-Anon's problems, growth and aspirations. They know, and can save us from, many unsuspected pitfalls we might blunder into, often through solutions worked out by trial and error in AA. Their wise help in the preparation of Al-Anon literature keeps it in character, unfailingly representing the ideas by which all of us are striving to live in Al-Anon.

"HQ serves as a clearing house for Al-Anon world-wide. Thousands of new situations, problems and answers are revealed by the letters received. This gives the Literature Committee a broad base of information for its guidance in selecting subjects to be covered, and in preparing the copy for them, making Conference-Approved literature valid for all Al-Anon. In addition, new information on alcoholism research is continually being funneled in

HQ, often suggesting ideas that keep our literature in step with modern advances.

"For all these reasons it is vital that we make full use of our Conference-Approved literature, which truly reflects our wonderful, growing fellowship. All of us are but leaves on a single, flourishing tree; offshoots can only weaken it!"

22. AA Literature on the Al-Anon Order Form:

The following text is from *First Steps* (p. 88): "The first Al-Anon price list distributed in September 1952, shows that Al-Anon sold the AA 'big book' and *AA Grapevine* subscriptions, besides the pamphlets already referred to." (p. 89) "By 1954, the Al-Anon literature list had expanded again. It included a subscription to *The Forum*, some new AA publications and reprints on alcoholism...."

The AA "big book" remained on the Al-Anon Family Group Publication 1956 order form; however, by November of 1959 it had been removed. Reprints from the AA *Grapevine* remained on the order forms for a few more years.

23. The Structure Of The Al-Anon Fellowship[141]

"Al-Anon is composed of two elements:

"1) The program which provides spiritual guidance and inspiration to its members, and

"2) the Al-Anon Services which maintain communications and take care of routine operations.

"The first is the spiritual core of the fellowship, embodied in The Twelve Steps, and The Twelve Traditions.[142]

"The Services are structured only to the extent that assures effective functioning and free exchange of information and help.

---

141. This chapter was added in March 1966
142. The spiritual core is also embodied in the Twelve Concepts of Service.

"The keystone of Al-Anon is the membership. It is made up of people who are closely associated, by ties of family or friendship, with compulsive drinkers.

"The basic unit is the Al-Anon group, which may consist of any two or more individuals who come together for mutual help.

"The operation of a group is the responsibility of a set of officers who are elected by the members. Officers are usually changed every three or six months, to give everyone an opportunity to serve. The officers are: a Chairman, a Secretary, a Program Chairman and a Treasurer. They have no authority over the group. Their functions are described in the next chapter.

"Thus far we have a picture of a self-contained unit, operating autonomously. How does the group, this one small cluster of individuals, play its role in the far-flung fellowship of Al-Anon which is made up of more than 4000[143] such groups? There are two major lines of communication.

"The first, consisting of some 3300[144] on the North American continent, are united in the World Service Conference.

"The second provision for communication is the World Service Office or Al-Anon Family Group Headquarters which acts as a service center for groups all over the world.

"The World Service Conference (WSC) was started on a trial basis in 1961 by agreement of the U.S. and Canadian membership. It proved so successful as a means of sharing experience and solving over-all problems that the Delegates decided, in 1963, to make the Conference a permanent feature of Al-Anon.

"The Delegates who meet at the annual WSC are elected in such a way that all groups share complete and equitable representation.

"Each group elects what is known as a Group Representative (GR).

---

143. The World Service Office has 29,800 Al-Anon and Alateen groups registered as of December 31, 1999.

144. The World Service Office has 18,000 groups registered in the U.S. and Canada as of December 31, 1999.

"The GR attends District meetings where problems are discussed and information is exchanged. A District is one segment of an Assembly Area in a State or Province. It is at the District meeting that the GRs elect a Committeeman[145] to represent the District.

"Committeemen and GRs are expected to attend all meetings of the Assembly when they are called by its Chairman. Once every three years they meet in the Assembly to elect, from among the Committeemen, the one who will serve as Delegate to the WSC for the ensuing three years.

"Each World Service Conference Delegate thus represents an Assembly, each Committeeman represents a District, each Group Representative a group.

"This succession of links gives each group a voice in the WSC.

"The same links provide a continuous chain of communication between the groups, the WSC and Headquarters; as streams of information and questions converge on the District meetings and through then to the Assembly and finally to the WSC, so the decisions of the Conference travel back through the same links from Delegate to Committeeman to Group Representative and thence to the group members.

"The WSC takes place annually. The Delegates bring up for consideration all current problems of the Al-Anon fellowship, questions and information which have been placed on the agenda for discussion by the Conference.

"The World Service Office (Headquarters) operates in conformity with the wishes of the fellowship as expressed by the Conference. It is represented at the sessions by members of the Board of Trustees, and the Executive and Policy Committees.

"The World Service Office is the principal service center of the fellowship. All the many functions and activities of the fellowship circulate through it. It is the center, not the head; it serves, but does

---

145. Currently referred to as district representative.

not control or direct. Work at WSO Headquarters is done by a small staff, assisted by a number of dedicated volunteers who share the huge volume of work, both creative and clerical. Thousands of inquiries are answered; new groups are given help in their early struggles and correspondence is maintained with the 4000 groups of the fellowship, as well as the lone members all over the world. Headquarters also takes care of over-all public relations, produces and ships all Conference Approved literature, as well as the monthly publication, *The Al-Anon Family Group Forum*[146], and looks after the voluminous details connected with the World Service Conference."

24. Application Of The Twelve Traditions to Group Problems

This chapter was written by Lois W. and added to the book in March 1966. The following is the updated version of the chapter as it has appeared since 1984.[147]

"When an Al-Anon group is formed, there is tacit agreement among the members that they will abide by the teaching of the fellowship. Those teachings, as they apply to the individual, are stated in the Twelve Steps; for the unity of the groups, in the Twelve Traditions.

"The Traditions are guides based on hard-won experience with group problems. They have served AA well; they serve Al-Anon equally well where there is willingness to learn what the Traditions mean and how to apply them. They give unfailing assurance of the survival and growth of the group.

"When three or four of us come together, we bring with us heartache, anxiety, shame, fear and confusion. We join forces in an Al-Anon group to help free ourselves from the problem that is depriving us of life, liberty and happiness.

"Study of the Twelve Traditions often reduces group problems to manageable size and points to logical, acceptable solutions. Many

---

146. The monthly magazine is now titled *The Forum*.

147. Assistance with group, district, and area problems can be found in the *Al-Anon/Alateen Service Manual*, "Policy Digest" section.

groups are able to find answers in the Digest of Al-Anon Policies,[148] a booklet containing guides and statements which have grown out of ongoing interpretations of the Twelve Traditions and our Twelve Concepts of Service.

"The Al-Anon World Service Office (WSO) receives letters each year from bewildered members who have encountered baffling group problems. Often they write in a desperate attempt to save a group that seems doomed to failure, sometimes because of the willfulness of a single member.

"Each of these letters is answered, and the answers are always based on one or more of the Twelve Traditions which Al-Anon adapted to its own needs from Alcoholics Anonymous.

Obedience to the Unenforceable

"We speak of the Traditions as guides. They are only that. They are not laws, rules, regulations or any other sort of compulsion. To those who are familiar with business or government, such lack of management control may be unthinkable.

"What, then, holds the Al-Anon fellowship together? What makes it grow and show such astounding results?

"It is based on a set of principles which its members use in solving problems related to alcoholism. Al-Anon derives its strength from *concentrating those principles on that one problem*. It holds together by means of a loving understanding among its members. Al-Anon is united—without organization, without management, without a chain of command or a set of rules—by its members' willingness *to be obedient to the unenforceable*.

"Willingly they struggle to face up to their personal problems and solve them with the help of the Twelve Steps of spiritual remotivation. Willingly they apply the Twelve Traditions to the affairs of the groups. Nobody compels them. They are learning to overcome selfwill, false pride, resentment and self-pity by recognizing that prin-

---

148. The Digest of Al-Anon Policies is now contained in the *Al-Anon/Alateen Service Manual*.

ciples are more important than personalities and by accepting a program on which they know they can depend for help.

Solving Group Problems

"These examples come from actual group experiences. In each instance the solution of the problem is found in one or more of the Traditions.

"a. The wife of a member of AA told, at an Al-Anon meeting, some of her husband's drinking episodes. What she said at the meeting was repeated by another member. Within days, this irresponsible gossiping came to the ears of the AA husband, led to a bitter falling out with his Al-Anon wife, caused dissension in the group, and ended by the husband's return to the bottle, with what he considered a good excuse.

"In reading Tradition Eleven we are encouraged to guard the anonymity of both Al-Anon and AA members. What is said at an Al-Anon meeting is said with the implicit promise that no word goes beyond the meeting room.

"This means we agree not to repeat anything said at a meeting, not even by referring to it in casual conversation *where it may seem quite harmless.*

"b. 'At our meetings we try to let each person around the table have a minute or so to talk on the subject of the meeting. But as soon as it gets around to one certain member, he gives a blow-by-blow description of all he has suffered from his wife's drinking. It always ends by his using up all the rest of the meeting time.'

"Our First Tradition says: 'Our *common welfare* should come first.' If one member monopolizes the time and attention of the group, the meeting is not serving the others. Some of those present are deprived of an opportunity to speak. Someone's helpful message may be lost. We must consider the welfare of the entire group. It does not even help the obsessive complainer to air his woes at such length. Perhaps more listening would give him some answers to his problem.

"The Chairman can interrupt courteously and ask the next person to make comments on the subject of the meeting, and can also emphasize, at the beginning of these round-the-table sessions, that each person has but one or two minutes to speak in order to give everyone an equal opportunity.

"c. 'Several members of our group seem more interested in planning social get-togethers like parties and picnics than in talking about Al-Anon. They resent it when some of the others remind them what we come to Al-Anon for...'

"According to Tradition Three, we are gathered together for mutual aid as *families of alcoholics*. Again, Tradition One says: 'personal progress depends on unity.'

"Al-Anon has unlimited possibilities *for helping us solve problems associated with alcoholism*, but when we go beyond that, we are not fulfilling our purpose. When two factions are disagreed on a situation like this, it is heading for disunity. We come to Al-Anon for help and solutions, and not for amusement. Individuals in the group may share social occasions; this has nothing to do with Al-Anon other than as a pleasant fringe benefit!

"d. 'Is it permissible for the alcoholic wife of an AA member to attend Al-Anon meetings?'

Tradition Five says our purpose is to help families of alcoholics. Because we make our meetings available to all who feel they are, or have been affected by someone else's drinking, many meetings are attended by recovering alcoholics. They are welcome and in addition to their own program, they may use Al-Anon to focus on family recovery.

"e. 'Several members of our group invariably decline to voice their thoughts and experiences at meetings. They say they are too shy—they'd rather listen to the others.'

"If we follow our First Tradition which reads: 'Our common welfare should come first,' it means that every Al-Anon member should use the privilege of helping the others in the group by participating.

"One member wrote: 'Remember, speaking is sharing your thoughts, your hopes, your strength and your weakness—it is the beginning of growth within you. You may just possess the key to someone's closed mind or heart. It is in giving that we receive. Only those who have shared their experiences with a problem can truly understand each other. If everyone would rather listen than speak, we would not have the active Al-Anon meetings we do, nor the books, nor the literature. All this is here today because so many have been unselfish.'

"f. 'Our group has always held its meetings in the evening. Recently some of the newer members suggested changing to a daytime hour. This is not convenient for the majority. Shouldn't the others go along with those of us who want to continue to meet in the evening?'

"Many members with young children find it difficult to attend meetings in the evening, when their youngsters need care and they can't afford baby sitters. Often it is impossible for them to attend Al-Anon meetings at all, particularly when active alcoholism in the home prevents them from leaving the children with someone who cannot be responsible for them. This leaves many free only during the hours when their children are in school.

"Shouldn't their welfare be considered too, under our First Tradition?

"The obvious solution is to suggest that those who want to meet in the daytime start another group, which they can then build up with others in a similar situation.

"This might be an opportunity for the existing group to put Al-Anon's philosophy of love into practice. They can help the new group get started and encourage them in every way to make it successful, by explaining Al-Anon procedures, providing some Conference-Approved Literature, and visiting the new group whenever possible. Under such conditions, what appears to be separation is really promoting Al-Anon unity.

"g. 'The Chairman of our group—she calls it MY group—permits no opposition to her ideas. Many newcomers drop off after one or two visits, although they need Al-Anon very much. She says it's because they're 'not ready'.'

"From our monthly publication, *The Forum*:

'A good Al-Anon group is the sum total of its members and not the property of a founder or a self-important Mr. or Mrs. Al-Anon.'

"According to our Second Tradition, no person in a group, information service (intergroup) or at the World Service Office, has authority to control or direct. An individual who assumes such authority should be set straight on the *equality* of all members of Al-Anon. An experienced, understanding older member of the group might speak to the offender privately and suggest that she allow leadership to rotate among the others in the group. Since such a personality is often difficult to persuade, stronger measures may have to be taken, perhaps ultimately to ask her to leave the group. Her desire to direct may stem from the best of motives, so anything that is said, or any action that is taken, should be motivated by patience, love and understanding.

In some instances the members of such a group have left it and re-formed without her. This course may be necessary if it cannot be handled in any other way, but it is, in a sense, running away from a problem that, with tact and kindness, could be solved without depriving the offending member of the benefits of Al-Anon membership.[149]

"h. 'We are enclosing a flyer describing what is termed an Al-Anon Retreat, to be held at one of our local churches. Although

---

149. One suggestion is to encourage a group to take an inventory. See guideline G-8, "Taking a Group Inventory."

it is the faith to which I belong, along with most of the members of our group, I have objected to this identification of Al-Anon with a specific church. Please help.'

"Traditionally, Al-Anon does not sponsor such gatherings, worthy and helpful though they may be. There can be no such thing as an Al-Anon Retreat, any more than there is an Al-Anon hospital, rest home or clinic.

"According to Tradition Three, we may call ourselves an Al-Anon group provided that, as a group, we have *no other affiliation*. Tradition Six says we ought never to endorse, finance or *lend our name to any outside enterprise*, lest we be diverted from our primary spiritual aim.

"The Al-Anon name cannot properly be used to identify or publicize retreats or any other activities sponsored by others. Even when most or all of the participants consider themselves members of Al-Anon, we should avoid anything that might cause public misunderstanding of our purpose or function.

"Experience has shown that no reference should be made to the participation of Al-Anon members in advance notices or reports. Even if an entire group wishes to attend the retreat, they do so as individuals, not as Al-Anon members.

"i. 'We have a problem which is going to be the ruination of our group which has been such a success in the past. One male member repeats everything we say at meetings to his AA wife, who then repeats them to the members of her AA group, many of whom are our husbands. Often the stories are so distorted and exaggerated as to be unrecognizable, which just makes it worse. This has led to a great deal of family dissension and several slips. We have had several serious talks with this member but he just laughs it off. What can we do?'

"If he is not responsive to your requests that he observe discretion about what goes on at your meetings, it might help to plan a meeting built on Tradition Five: 'Each Al-Anon group has but one purpose: to help families of alcoholics. We do this by practicing the Twelve Steps of AA ourselves, by encouraging and understanding our alcoholic relatives and by welcoming and giving comfort to families of alcoholics.'

"If even a single member causes difficulties for the families of alcoholics, your group cannot fully serve its purpose. Gossip destroys the very thing we join forces to achieve—serenity, acceptance and growth.

"Meetings can be planned where each participant is assigned one angle of the problem for discussion. Members can speak frankly about what can happen in a family as a result of such careless gossip.

"Some groups have an older member explain in private to the offending member that he may be impeding his own recovery by his unguarded talk.

"If all this fails, for the 'greatest good of the greatest number,' he may have to be warned and asked to leave the group if he continues to ignore the spiritual counsel of the Fifth Tradition.

"j. 'A friend of one of our members, a wealthy and generous woman who has long been interested in alcoholism as a social problem, has offered us a gift of one thousand dollars. She is convinced that we can attract many more members through newspaper announcements and widespread distribution of our literature, and that such a gift, in Al-Anon's hands, would do a great deal of good. How can we refuse without offending her?'

"The Seventh Tradition simply states that we should be fully self-supporting and decline outside contributions. There are excellent reasons for this.

"Perhaps she might not be hurt if it was explained that our growth must come from within. Al-Anon members should not be deprived of the privilege of supporting their own fellowship. Even the difficulties we face, and they are many, are wholesome disciplines.

Early experience of both AA and Al-Anon has been the guide in establishing this Tradition. Although this generous donor would surely not attempt to influence or control, we would, by accepting her gift, set a precedent that might mean selling our independence. Other individuals and organizations who might want to use the united influence of Al-Anon could try to establish their right by making substantial contributions.

"Our groups need only enough money to defray expenses for rent, literature, refreshments and contributions to the WSO and the area world service assembly. Every group should be able to take care of these modest obligations.

"Funds needed by an information service[150] should come from the groups concerned. They are responsible for its support, just as it is responsible for providing service and liaison between prospective members and the groups.

"If the Al-Anon WSO were to accept contributions from outsiders—and they are occasionally offered—it would change the entire structure of the fellowship. It would affect the close relationship between the WSO and the groups.

"It is an abiding condition of the Al-Anon fellowship that its members support their groups and the groups support the WSO, which uses these funds to provide world-wide service. This interdependence is a wholesome and sustaining condition, preserving all Al-Anon in unity and equality.

"k. A member of our group, deeply interested in civil rights, tries to persuade the other members to take part in demonstrations.

"There are many worthy causes of interest to some or all of the members of a group. But our only concern, as Al-Anon members, is to help ourselves and others to live with the problem of alcoholism.

"Tradition Ten states that the Al-Anon Family Groups take no stand on outside issues.

---

150. Information service refers to Al-Anon information service (AIS) or intergroup.

Individually we are free to do anything we wish to about other causes and organizations, but not as an Al-Anon group.

"A member of another group, interested in a foundling home, feels that the group should help a cause so worthy. And there is a certain elementary logic in her position; as human beings, striving to better ourselves and the world, we are moved and concerned for the welfare of others. But if Al-Anon were to involve itself in every worthwhile cause, where could we draw the line that would keep our fellowship intact to do its job?

"The Traditions wisely suggest that Al-Anon groups devote themselves to Al-Anon's purpose.

"1. 'We have a member who is separated from her alcoholic husband and has the care of four small children. We know she is having a hard time getting along; several of us have given her money from time to time. At our last business meeting someone brought up the question of helping her by giving her a few dollars from the group contributions each week. Some of us do not agree that this should be done. What's the answer?'

"What would the answer be if there were more members in equal need? Could the group afford to help them all and still fulfill its primary purpose, which it does by supporting the expense of meeting, and by providing literature for those who need emotional and spiritual help?

"Distress cases occur fairly frequently in Al-Anon groups; once a group has helped a needy family, it has established a precedent. How can it then refuse to help others in need? It is not the responsibility of the group to act as a welfare organization; many social agencies are equipped and financed for this.

"Tradition Five describes the purposes of Al-Anon; to help families of alcoholics by practicing the Twelve Steps of AA ourselves, by encouraging and understanding our alcoholic relatives and by welcoming and giving comfort to families of alcoholics. This does not include giving financial aid *as a group*.

"Individuals who wish to give or lend money to others may, of course, do so, but funds contributed to the group should be used only for group obligations.

"m. Questions frequently arise that call for clarification of the relationship of Al-Anon and AA.

1. Should AA literature be displayed at Al-Anon meetings?

2. Should some groups which meet in the same building as an AA group and get together with them afterward provide the refreshments for these occasions?

3. Should Al-Anon groups provide funds for starting an AA group, paying rent, providing refreshments and even buying a stock of literature?

"Tradition Six says in part: 'we ought never finance any outside enterprise' and concludes with 'although a separate entity, we should always cooperate with AA.'

1) AA literature is readily available at an AA meeting. Neither fellowship makes it a practice to stock or distribute the other's literature.

2) If the Al-Anon group regularly pays for joint refreshments, it is financing AA's share of this obligation unless, of course, it is Al-Anon's way of paying rent for a meeting room. The funds contributed to AA are used to defray AA expenses; those that are contributed to Al-Anon are used for Al-Anon purposes.

3) Finally, for an Al-Anon group to help an AA group get started is definitely an intrusion into the affairs of a separate fellowship, which is covered in Tradition Six. Close as we are to AA—we do not take over AA's responsibilities or activities. AA is just as dedicated to solving the problems of the alcoholic as we are to solving those of the alcoholic's family; our two functions should remain separate.

"In all our relations with AA we should be guided not by rigid rules, but by common sense. Where finances are concerned, most

Al-Anon groups have all they can do to meet their own obligations with the funds contributed at their meetings. Financial involvements on either side can create awkward situations.

"There have been many instances when AA has helped a struggling Al-Anon group, but every effort should be made to become and remain self-supporting.

"n. A group in need of more funds than are provided by its regular contributions asks whether the idea of a public raffle would be acceptable.

"Two of the Traditions question this idea.

"Tradition Seven says that every group ought to be fully self-supporting. If this raffle yields a profit, as it is intended to do, we are accepting help from others for the support of Al-Anon.

"Tradition Eleven concerns anonymity at the level of press, radio, TV and films. But most AA newcomers and many AA and Al-Anon groups take their anonymity much further. Therefore it would be inconsiderate for Al-Anon members to engage in such an enterprise.

"The proposed raffle could, of course, be undertaken if only Al-Anon and AA members were involved.[151]

"o. A State Alcohol Committee has enlisted the aid of various local organizations in helping alcoholics and their families. One of these is the local Al-Anon group, which agreed to cooperate, and undertook to pay part of the cost of circularizing a mailing list.

"This activity is questionable on the basis of a number of Al-Anon Traditions.

"First, Al-Anon would appear to the public to have affiliated itself with the local Committee on Alcoholism. Our Third Tradition states that we may call ourselves an Al-Anon group 'provided that, as a group, we have; no other affiliation.'

---

151. See Policy Digest, Finances, Fund-Raising section, *Al-Anon/Alateen Service Manual.*

"Second, Tradition Six states that 'we ought never endorse, finance, or lend our name to any outside enterprise, lest problems of money, property or prestige divert us from our primary spiritual aim.' The letter gives the impression that the Alcoholism Committee considers Al-Anon merely a branch of AA or the sponsoring Committee or both. Al-Anon is not under the sponsorship of any Committee.

"Third, it also put the Al-Anon group under obligation to support the Committee's activities, whether or not they conform to Al-Anon ideas and standards.

"Such a concerted effort may make it possible to reach many more people than Al-Anon could by itself. Breaking Traditions, however, may result in accomplishing immediate good at the cost of lessening Al-Anon's future usefulness by submerging its identity or diverting it from its purpose.

"p. From time to time a group may question certain activities of another group which it feels is violating our Eleventh Tradition: 'Our public relations policy is based on attraction rather than promotion.' Among the practices to which objection has been voiced are the following:

1. Announcing in a newspaper the formation of an Al-Anon group, or publishing the time and place of a group's meeting.

2. Mention of the Al-Anon fellowship on TV or radio, even when no names are given and no persons can be identified.

3. Working with 'outsiders'—clergymen, doctors and social workers—to interest them in Al-Anon as a source of help for families who consult them about problems connected with alcoholism.

4. The use of a conspicuous book jacket on an Al-Anon book.

"These objections may be due to misunderstanding of several of the Traditions. The Fifth states: 'Each Al-Anon group has but one purpose: to help families of alcoholics.' This Tradition ends with the words: 'by welcoming and giving comfort to families of alcoholics.'

"We welcome and help by making it known that there is such a fellowship as Al-Anon. Whatever we can do *that does not violate the anonymity of an individual* is permissible, provided, of course, that it is kept on a serious and dignified level.

"We try to reach as many of these troubled families as we can. Our Twelfth-Step work is not limited to those who have been fortunate enough to hear about Al-Anon accidentally. We have a message to carry.

"When our Eleventh Tradition says; 'Our public relations policy is based on attraction rather than promotion,' it suggests we should not hesitate to attract to it anyone who needs the help of Al-Anon.

"There are many acceptable ways of attracting people to Al-Anon without promotion. We can feel perfectly free to inform others who work in the field of alcoholism about Al-Anon. These include individual professionals who are consulted by people in trouble, as well as state, provincial and local councils and associations working with alcoholism problems, churches, hospitals, and, of course, AA.[152]

"q. 'The AA group in our neighborhood is favorable to Al-Anon and has encouraged the spouses of its members to start a group. We hesitate because we feel we cannot afford the initial expense, and rent, refreshments and literature. The AA group has offered to provide the money to start with. Shall we accept it?'

"It is traditional, in both AA and Al-Anon, not to enter into financial involvements, whether to accept or give help. According to Tradition Seven, every group should be fully self-supporting.

On that basis it would not be desirable to accept the generous offer make by the AA group.

"There are two alternatives:

If the prospective members cannot start out with enough money to cover one month's rent and a small stock of literature, funds to

---

152. See the *Al-Anon/Alateen Service Manual* and the guidelines G-1—G-34 for guidance and ideas on outreach to the public and professionals.

cover these expenses might be borrowed from a member or members, with the understanding that it will be repaid as promptly as possible.

It might be better for the group at first to limit its expenditure for literature to the minimum. When a group is financially able, it can spread its wings a little, pay for a meeting place, order a more adequate stock of literature and set some money aside for its contributions to WSO and the Area Assembly.

"The offer of the AA group has a greater significance than the merely financial; such whole-hearted interest could mean an early and substantial membership for the new group which would enable it to stand on its own feet.

"r. 'One of our members is acquainted with the author of an inspirational book which has had some acceptance. She would like to invite this author to give a talk at one of our meetings and to autograph copies of her book of which she would bring along a number of copies to sell. Some of us are opposed to this because the book is not directly connected with Al-Anon or alcoholism.'

"While it is certainly in order to invite outsiders to speak at an Al-Anon meeting occasionally, it should be someone who is familiar with the problems of the families of alcoholics. That is Al-Anon's primary concern.

"This situation, as the member describes it, involves Tradition Six which says we ought never endorse, finance or lend our name to any outside enterprise. This we would be doing in having the book offered for sale at an Al-Anon meeting.

"s. 'We are a metropolitan group consisting largely of successful career women. Whatever problems we have, shortage of funds is not among them.

'One faction is very much interested in engaging the services of a psychiatric counselor who would attend our meetings and help advise us on our problems. The opposing faction feels that this does not fit into the Al-Anon program.

'We need impartial advice.'

"The answer comes, of course, directly from our Traditions. 'Our Twelfth-Step work should remain forever non-professional, although our service centers may employ special workers.'

"The task proposed for the counselor would essentially be Twelfth-Step work which, in Al-Anon, is performed by members who share and understand the problems that plague those whose lives are disturbed by compulsive drinking. The exception mentioned in the Eighth Tradition refers only to office workers who take care of the business of the service centers.

"Professional and personal advice is not part of the Al-Anon program. Members desiring such advice may seek it elsewhere, but not at an Al-Anon meeting.

25. The Twelve Concepts of Service

The Twelve Concepts of Service were approved in 1970 by the World Service Conference and given the same stature as the Twelve Steps and Twelve Traditions in 1984. The Concepts are now published in *Al-Anon Family Groups* for the first time.

Al-Anon's Twelve Concepts Of Service

Carrying the message, as suggested in the Twelfth Step, is Service, Al-Anon's third legacy. Service, a vital purpose of Al-Anon, is *action*. Members strive to *do* as well as to *be*.

Anything done to help a relative or friend of an alcoholic is service: a telephone call to a despairing member or sponsoring a newcomer, telling one's story at meetings, forming groups, arranging for public information, distributing literature, and financially supporting groups, local services and the World Service Office.

1. The ultimate responsibility and authority for Al-Anon world services belongs to the Al-Anon groups.

2. The Al-Anon Family Groups have delegated complete administrative and operational authority to their Conference and its service arms.

3. The Right of Decision makes effective leadership possible.

4. Participation is the key to harmony.

5. The Rights of Appeal and Petition protect minorities and assure that they be heard.

6. The Conference acknowledges the primary administrative responsibility of the trustees.

7. The trustees have legal rights while the rights of the Conference are traditional.

8. The Board of Trustees delegates full authority for routine management of the Al-Anon Headquarters to its executive committees.

9. Good personal leadership at all service levels is a necessity. In the field of world service the Board of Trustees assumes the primary leadership.

10. Service responsibility is balanced by carefully defined service authority and double-headed management is avoided.

11. The World Service Office is composed of standing committees, executives and staff members.

12. The spiritual foundation for Al-Anon's world service is contained in the General Warranties of the Conference, Article 12 of the Charter.

GENERAL WARRANTIES

In all its proceedings the World Service Conference of Al-Anon shall observe the spirit of the Traditions:

1. that only sufficient operating funds, including an ample reserve, be its prudent financial principle;

2. that no Conference member shall be placed in unqualified authority over other members;

3. that all decisions be reached by discussion, vote and, whenever possible, by unanimity;

4. that no Conference action ever be personally punitive or an incitement to public controversy;

5. that though the Conference serves Al-Anon, it shall never perform any act of government; and that, like the fellowship of Al-Anon Family Groups which it serves, it shall always remain democratic in thought and action.[153]

26. AA and Al-Anon Slogans[154]

"Slogans that became traditional in AA have been gratefully taken over by many Al-Anon groups. Their recall and interpretation often makes the basis of worthwhile discussions at Al-Anon meetings. Below are some of the most cherished slogans:

> First Things First
> Easy Does It
> Live and Let Live
> But For the Grace of God
> Let Go and Let God
> Just For Today

---

153. For additional information on the Twelve Concepts of Service, see the *Al-Anon/Alateen Service Manual* (P-24/27), *The Concepts: Al-Anon's Best Kept Secret?* (P-57) and *Paths to Recovery: Al-Anon's Steps, Traditions, and Concepts* (B-24).

154. This chapter was introduced to the book in March 1960. Later the chapter was retitled, "The Slogans of Al-Anon."

First Things First

"Sometimes in our enthusiasm to get things going in this new way of life we don't know where to begin; there are so many things that need to be done, so many areas to tackle. If we just sit down and think out which is the first and most important thing, the less important things usually fall into place. If, for instance, we can see that our own integrity is the most important thing, our husband's sobriety and the children's best welfare may also follow. What might appear without careful thought as a selfish attitude is seen to be the first and most important thing, benefiting others as well as ourselves.

Easy Does It

"We Al-Anon members often expect too much too soon. We expect too much of our alcoholics, after they have joined AA, and of ourselves. So easy does it. Take it a day at a time. Living the AA and Al-Anon program is a lifetime job. Making a start with sincerity and steady progress is what counts. Pushing our alcoholics or ourselves leads to frustrations and tensions, just the things we are trying to avoid.

Live and Let Live

"Along with the release of tension that Al-Anon brings is a more reasonable attitude toward trying to manage other people's lives. We come to believe that *our* way to a more serene outlook may not be the solution for the alcoholic, our relatives and friends, or other members of Al-Anon. We try to improve ourselves rather than criticize the rest of the world.

But For the Grace of God

"No matter how deeply scientists may analyze AA, there is always an "X" factor which they cannot explain. The grace of God is indeed behind the miracles of recovery. Less dramatically but just as effectively, the grace of God is behind our own recoveries in

Al-Anon. The more we open our hearts to its influx the greater and the faster will our recoveries be.

Keep an Open Mind

"Set aside any prejudices or doubts you may have about what Al-Anon can do for you. Don't judge the group or the program by one or two meetings. Sooner or later a member will say something that reaches your heart as well as your mind. Keep an open mind about alcoholism as a disease by learning all you can about it. Go to as many AA meetings as possible; they will clear a mental pathway for new concepts about all alcoholics, and especially yours. Keep an open mind about the Twelve Steps; they can fill you with hope and serenity.

Let Go and Let God

"This is a guide to better living. When we turn our wills and our lives over to the care of God, we get rid of conflicts within ourselves created through self-centeredness.

"After taking our moral inventory, we have a desire to be different. When we admit this to God, He will take over. As we begin to change, our faith grows. As our faith grows, our fears and tensions will go.

"Every day we have decisions to make and problems to overcome. If we supply the willingness, God supplies the power. Through this way of living, we grow spiritually. At the end of each day we find that serenity has come through letting go and letting God.

Just for Today

"Just for today I will try to live through this day only, and not tackle my whole life problem at once. I can do something for twelve hours that would appall me if I felt that I had to keep it up for a lifetime.

"Just for today I will be happy. Abraham Lincoln said, 'Most folks are as happy as they make up their minds to be.'

"Just for today I will adjust myself to what is, and not try to adjust everything to my own desires. I will take my luck as it comes, and fit myself to it.

"Just for today I will try to strengthen my mind. I will study. I will exercise my soul in three ways: I will do somebody a good turn, and not get found out; if anybody knows of it, it will not count. I will do something I don't want to do, just for the exercise. I will not show anyone when my feelings are hurt.

"Just for today I will be agreeable. I will look as well as I can, dress becomingly, talk low, act courteously, criticize not one bit, not find fault with anything, and not try to improve or regulate anybody but myself.

"Just for today I will have a program. I may not follow it exactly, but I will have it. I will save myself from two pests: hurry and indecision.

"Just for today I will have a quiet time all by myself, and relax. During this half hour, sometime, I will try to get a better perspective of my life.

"Just for today I will be unafraid. Especially I will not be afraid to enjoy what is beautiful, and to believe that as I give to the world so the world will give to me."

27. Talk Given By Bill W., Co-founder of Alcoholics Anonymous to the First World Service Conference April 1961 [155]

"First on behalf of AAs everywhere, I want to bring to this gathering our congratulations and deep affection. There was a time when I could not have done this with equanimity. Many AAs were afraid you were going to crash our exclusive club! But the success of Al-Anon has not only been phenomenal, but I feel it is just about the best thing that has happened since AA began.

---

155. This chapter was added to the appendix of the book in March 1966.

"I know you have approached this new venture with trepidation and misgiving. You have wondered if this Conference will work, if Delegates will really come from the far reaches of Canada and the United States, and how they will work together if they do come. What will the spirit of the Conference be?

"These were questions we in AA asked ourselves when *we* held our first General Service Conference in 1951. But our Conference *was* a success and it has continued to have force and effect in all the years since. Sensing the spirit of this meeting, I am sure this will also be the case with you.

"In growth, as movement, you have exceeded anything that ever happened to AA in its early years. And this is, as we all know, because you have been intent on filing the vast vacuum that has so long existed in family relations. We alcoholics, on getting sober, were quickly able to get back to some sort of job. Now there is a little money in the bank; we are madly active in AA. We make restitution to everybody in the world except the people we have really mauled, and those people are your good selves.

"For a long time we all wondered why this 'honeymoon' didn't resume. We would say to the wife: 'This AA is great stuff; come over to our meetings and get a load of it. We'll even allow you to make the coffee while you warm you hands at the spiritual fires of Alcoholics Anonymous.'

"Happily, all of that is now in the past; you are commencing to fill, with tremendous rapidity and effect, that awful vacuum that has existed all along, which has affected half of our membership in this close family relation. Of course the family relation is the most difficult one because it's the one that has been the most deformed.

"So we AAs, along with our affection and congratulations, do bring you our deep regret, as well as what little restitution we can make at this late date, for the emotional disturbances that our drinking days imposed upon you.

"Now comes the time when Al-Anon must function as a whole. You have a dedicated group here. Naturally they had to be self-appointed in the beginning—that was the only way they could get things started. As Doctor Bob and I were known to all AA, so are Lois and her associates here known to you. But this is too thin a linkage for the future. Your services, so vital to the spread of Al-Anon though out the world, must now be a function of Al-Anon as a whole.

"So the deep significance of this small but wonderful meeting, in which history is about to repeat itself, is this: that you are now applying Tradition Two to Al-Anon as a whole. You Delegates, who have come here as Al-Anon's group conscience, are trusted servants.

"True, prodigies of work can be done by mail; prodigies of work can be done through literature. Yet basically it is here, as in AA, that you must finally transact your affairs face-to-face. Now you are face-to-face with your old-timers, your veterans in Al-Anon's service. You have now become the conscience and guide of Al-Anon, and that is a forward step of the greatest significance, something that should give you deep satisfaction.

"Let me emphasize the perils that would surely have beset you had you not begun so to gather. I keep going back to our AA experience. Like yourselves, we AAs had had a Trusteeship, a center of service in New York that spread AA throughout the world. People used to say: 'Well, this is fine, and it is simple. We'll send in money and you folks will do the work.' Therefore when a General Service Conference was proposed for AA, people said: 'My God, we drunks can't even run a clubhouse; why should we now risk thirty elections of Delegates each year when things are really going along so well?'

"But some of us did realize that the old-timers who operated the AA services could not last forever. We old-timers are getting to be old-timers not only in AA years but in natural years. Many of us have only five, ten or fifteen years to go before we cross the Great

Divide. We had to recognize that Tradition Two had to have the true meaning for the movement as a whole. Hence we recognized that a linkage—a permanent linkage—had to be built between the AA group conscience and its world operations. Thank God you Al-Anons are now seeing that you must do the same. Otherwise a possible future breakdown at your world center could never be repaired. There would be no way to reinstate those vital services unless the Delegate's linkage existed, the kind of linkage you are creating on this historic occasion—the inauguration of your first World Service Conference.

"Sometimes you Delegates will come here to give advice; indeed it is in your power to give active direction because the ultimate authority is yours. Then again you will offer suggestions that will make for greater progress. Sometimes you will face momentous questions and problems in which your guidance and collective wisdom will surely manifest itself and save you from grievous error.

"At other times you will come here and find internal troubles and you will correct these. At still other times you will have Conference meetings which will be so boring, so dull, that some of you may say: 'Why in Heaven's name go to New York just to say 'Yes' to what our public accountant has already verified? This is a lot of nonsense!' But no matter what happens, your presence will insure the maintenance of the all important linkage. Each one of these yearly meetings, be they dull, be they controversial, is really the insurance policy which can guarantee the future unity and functioning of your society.

"May God bless and keep you all. May He set His special favor upon this auspicious beginning. You will surely look back upon this day as a great one in the annals of the Al-Anon Family Groups."

28. Other Historical Notes and Timeline re: *Al-Anon Family Groups*

Historical notes

Archival research of the original text and subsequent editions have revealed the following interesting tidbits of information:

The Al-Anon World Service Office was first referred to as "the Clearing House." The office was later referred to as "Headquarters" and subsequently as the "World Service Office" (WSO).

Subtitles for the book have also changed throughout the years. In the first edition the title reads, "The Al-Anon Family Groups—A Guide for Families of Problem Drinkers." Later editions stated, "A Program for .. " and "A Way of Life for the Families of Problem Drinkers." When the book was retitled *Living With An Alcoholic,* the subtitle was "with the help of Al-Anon." Upon retitling once again, the book remained *Al-Anon Family Groups* with the subtitle of the former title, "Living With An Alcoholic."

Total production costs in 1955 for the first edition printing of 5,000 copies were $3,000. The publisher graciously allowed Al-Anon to pay in four installments; however, payment was made in three.

The "Historical Forward" typed in one of the first draft manuscripts was first titled "Alcoholics and the Non-Alcoholic." Lois noted on it "poor title." Similar comments and changes were found throughout the development of the "pamphlet."

By comparing the various publications over the years, we learned that members "stories" or "sharings" also played an important role in carrying the Al-Anon message to readers. Some stories were totally removed, others remained the same with no edits; others were revised (it appears) by the original writers.

In 1979 The Literature Committee considered reprinting *Al-Anon Family Groups* "...to be used as a commemorative piece or a nostalgic item for a special occasion. The committee recognized the high cost involved and suggested that its value as a memorabilia item would be enhanced by the passage of more time."

29. Chronological printing history of *Al-Anon Family Groups*

Throughout the years the chapters of the book have been moved to varying locations. Tracking of each move is not documented.

1. June 1955—First Printing, First Edition

2. March 1956—Second Printing, First Edition

3. May 25, 1957—Copyright registered with Library of Congress

4. September 1958—Third Printing, First Edition

5. March 1960—Revision—*Al-Anon Family Groups*—Al-Anon's basic book, revised, enlarged and published as *Living With An Alcoholic*. Second Edition

October 10, 1961 Directors Meeting Minutes:

"A letter was received from Cornwall Press inquiring if we expected to have any further use for the plates for the original book, *The Al-Anon Family Groups*. All members agreeing that it was unlikely that there would be any reason for reprinting the original book.

"A motion was made by Lois and seconded by Vi and unanimously carried that we authorize Cornwall Press to destroy the plates for the first book."

6. January 1962—2nd printing, Second Edition

7. April 1964—3rd printing, Second Edition

8. March 1966—Third Edition

9. June 1968—2nd printing, Third Edition

10. November 1971—3rd printing, Third Edition

11. May 1973 (revised)—4th Edition (numbering sequence did not start over)

Second Copyright registered with Library of Congress

12. July 1974—5th printing

13. January 1976—6th printing

14. September 1976—7th printing

15. March 1978 (revised)—8th printing

16. March 1980 (revised)—9th printing

Third Copyright registered with the Library of Congress

17. April 1981—10th printing

18. November 1982—11th printing

19. March 1984—12th printing (1983—*Living With An Alcoholic*—reverts to its original title, *Al-Anon Family Groups*)

Fourth Copyright registered with the Library of Congress

20. February 1985—13th printing

21. February 1986—14th printing

22. November 1987—15th printing

23. 1989—16th printing

24. 1991—17th printing

25. July 1995—18th printing (1st printing in soft cover; book is printed with 17th printing in code—in error)

26. July 2000 - 26th printing. (1st reprinting of original text with footnotes and Appendix II)

Fifth Copyright registered with Library of Congress

Note: Only substantial changes are presented in footnotes or the Appendix II for this 26th printing of *The Al-Anon Family Groups*. Minor changes in other editions are not documented.

Index